GIVING TO GOD

Dr. David Jeremiah

with Dr. David Jeremiah

CONTENTS

ABOUT
DR. DAVID JEREMIAH
AND TURNING POINT

D r. David Jeremiah is the founder of Turning Point, a ministry committed to providing Christians with sound Bible teaching relevant to today's changing times through radio and television broadcasts, audio series, and books. Dr. Jeremiah's common-sense teaching on topics such as family, prayer, worship, angels, and biblical prophecy forms the foundation of Turning Point.

David and his wife, Donna, reside in El Cajon, California, where he is the senior pastor of Shadow Mountain Community Church and chancellor of San Diego Christian College. David and Donna have four children and eight grandchildren.

In 1982, Dr. Jeremiah brought the same solid teaching to San Diego television that he shares weekly with his congregation. Shortly thereafter, Turning Point expanded its ministry to radio. Dr. Jeremiah's inspiring messages can now be heard worldwide on radio and television.

Because Dr. Jeremiah desires to know his listening audience, he travels nationwide holding "A Night of Encouragement" ministry rallies and Spiritual Enrichment conferences that touch the hearts and lives of many people. According to Dr. Jeremiah, "At some point in time, everyone reaches a turning point; and for every person, that moment is unique, an experience to hold onto forever. There's so much changing in today's world that sometimes it's difficult to choose the right path. Turning Point offers people an understanding of God's Word as well as the opportunity to make a difference in their lives."

Dr. Jeremiah has authored numerous books, including *Escape the Coming Night* (Revelation), *The Handwriting on the Wall* (Daniel), *Overcoming Loneliness, What the Bible Says About Angels, The Joy of Encouragement, Prayer—The Great Adventure, God in You* (Holy Spirit), *Gifts from God* (Parenting), *Jesus' Final Warning, When Your World Falls Apart, Slaying the Giants in Your Life, My Heart's Desire, Sanctuary, Life Wide Open, Searching for Heaven on Earth, The Secret of the Light, Captured by Grace, Discover Paradise, Grace Givers,* and *Why the Nativity.*

ABOUT THIS
STUDY GUIDE

The purpose of this Turning Point study guide is to reinforce Dr. David Jeremiah's dynamic, in-depth teaching on *Giving to God* and to aid the reader in applying biblical truth to his or her daily life. This study guide is designed to be used in conjunction with Dr. Jeremiah's *Giving to God* audio series, but it may be used by itself for personal or group Bible study.

STRUCTURE OF THE LESSONS

Each lesson is based on one of the messages in the *Giving to God* audio series and focuses on specific passages in the Bible. Each lesson is composed of the following elements:

• *Outline*

The outline at the beginning of the lesson gives a clear, concise picture of the passage being studied and provides a helpful framework for readers as they listen to Dr. Jeremiah's teaching.

• *Overview*

The overview summarizes Dr. Jeremiah's teaching on the passage being studied in the lesson. Readers should refer to the biblical passages in their own Bibles as they study the overview.

• *Application*

This section contains a variety of questions designed to help readers dig deeper into the lesson and the Scriptures, and to apply the lesson to their daily lives. For Bible study groups or Sunday school classes, these questions will provide a springboard for group discussion and interaction.

• *Did You Know?*

This section presents a fascinating fact, historical note, or insight that adds a point of interest to the preceding lesson.

USING THIS GUIDE FOR GROUP STUDY

The lessons in this study guide are suitable for Sunday school classes, small-group studies, elective Bible studies, or home Bible study groups. Each person in the group should have his or her own study guide.

When possible, the study guide should be used with the corresponding audio series. You may wish to assign the study guide as homework prior to the meeting of the group and then use the meeting time to listen to the message and discuss the lesson.

FOR CONTINUING STUDY

A complete catalog of Dr. Jeremiah's materials for personal and group study is available through Turning Point. To obtain a catalog, additional study guides, or more information about Turning Point, call 1-800-947-1993 or write to: Turning Point, P.O. Box 3838, San Diego, CA 92163.

Dr. Jeremiah's *Turning Point* program is currently heard or viewed around the world on radio, television, and the Internet in English. *Momento Decisivo,* the Spanish translation of Dr. Jeremiah's messages, can be heard on radio in every Spanish speaking country in the world. In some areas the television broadcast is translated into the Russian language.

Contact Turning Point for radio and television program times and stations in your area. Or visit our website at www.turningpointonline.org.

GIVING TO
GOD

INTRODUCTION

In the summer of 1996, a man named Joe from Janesville, Wisconsin, received a check from the Social Security Administration for $40,945. Joe was entitled to the money, but he was not supposed to have received it directly. Instead, it was supposed to have been sent to a person who was responsible for Joe's finances. That's because Joe has an IQ of about seventy and suffers from bouts of manic depression. Compounding Joe's personal limitations was the fact that Joe was unemployed and had a gambling problem.

Joe's windfall became his undoing. Whenever he felt down or depressed he'd go on a gambling binge at a nearby casino. Because Joe often felt depressed, the money didn't last long. In a matter of weeks, he had blown the entire $41,000.

The sad part of Joe's story is that he hadn't wanted to waste the money. He had planned to use it to buy a house and provide for the three children he had fathered. Because Joe didn't have the skills necessary to manage such a large amount of money, the good things the money might have accomplished went unrealized.

In many ways, all of us are like Joe when it comes to money. In our fallen state, our natural inclination, and often our practice, is to spend everything we have on ourselves. And if we don't have the actual money, we'll use credit cards to extend our buying power beyond our ability. Most people don't make the mistake Joe made—gambling the money away or spending it on other frivolous pursuits. But regardless of how we spend it, we think our money is exactly that: ours. Without a guide or advisor—someone more mature and responsible than we are—we might get to the end of our life and look back and wonder what we did with all we had.

Fortunately, the Bible says that those who know God have such an advisor—the Holy Spirit. Through the wisdom imparted by the Spirit of God, we come to learn something that is the exact opposite of what we thought before. Instead of thinking that everything we have is ours, we learn that nothing we have is ours. The Bible calls this revelation "stewardship"—the understanding that God owns everything and that what we have is given by God for us to manage on earth for His glory.

The concept of Christian stewardship, like all other areas of biblical teaching, runs counter to the philosophy of this world. For the Christian, money is not an end in itself but a means to an end—a way to provide for our basic needs and to invest eternally in the program and purpose of God on earth.

The title of this study guide, *Giving to God*, reflects one of the key principles in God's economy: As we give to God, He gives to us in the same degree. Or, in the words of the apostle Paul, we reap what we sow (Galatians 6:7). As we faithfully manage the resources God entrusts to us, He gives us even more. God's harvest law promises that as we are obedient and generous with what we have, God will provide an abundant supply whereby we may continue to meet our own needs and those of others.

The ten lessons in this study guide provide an overview of all the fundamental aspects of Christian financial stewardship: basic principles, tithing, how God measures giving, the necessity for teaching about money from the pulpit, the nature of sacrifice, God's harvest law, and others.

Whether you are new to the faith or have been a Christian for years, *Giving to God* will serve as a thorough introduction or timely review of how to make the most of what God has entrusted to you.

MEET THE "STEWARD" OF STEWARDSHIP

Genesis 24

*In this lesson we are introduced
to the idea of stewardship.*

OUTLINE

If you could record your conversations for a day, you might be surprised at how often you use the word "my." In truth, we own nothing. Everything we have has come from God and belongs to Him. Our role is to be a faithful manager on earth of what has come to us from heaven.

I. Aspects of Stewardship
   A. Accountability
   B. Availability
   C. Anxiousness
   D. Allegiance
   E. Agreeableness
   F. Attributing Praise

II. Concepts of Stewardship

III. Principles of Stewardship
   A. God Owns Everything
   B. We Are God's Administrators
   C. How We Administer Determines How God Distributes
   D. We Shall All Give an Account Someday

Perhaps you can identify with this letter that someone wrote in response to an appeal for a financial contribution:

"In reply to your request to send a check, I wish to inform you that the present condition of my bank account makes it almost impossible. My shattered financial condition is due to the federal laws, the state laws, the county laws, the corporation laws, the mother-in-laws, the sister-in-laws, and the outlaws. Through these laws, I am compelled to pay a business tax, an amusement tax, a head tax, a school tax, a gas tax, a light tax, a water tax, and a sales tax. Even my brains are taxed.

"I am required to get a business license, a dog license, a truck license, not to mention a marriage license. I'm also required to contribute to every organization or society which the genius of man is capable of bringing to life—women's relief, unemployment relief, every hospital and charitable organization in the city, including the Red Cross, the Black Cross, the Purple Cross, and the double-cross.

"For my own safety, I am required to carry insurance: property insurance, life insurance, liability insurance, burglary insurance, accident insurance, business insurance, earthquake insurance, tornado insurance, unemployment insurance, old age insurance, and fire insurance. I am respected, inspected, expected, disrespected, rejected, dejected, examined, reexamined, informed, reformed, summoned, fined, commanded, and compelled until I supply an inexhaustible supply of money for every known need, desire, or hope of the human race.

"Simply because I refuse to donate something or another, I am boycotted, talked about, lied about, held up, held down, robbed until I'm ruined. I can tell you honestly that had not the unexpected happened, I could not enclose this check. The wolf that comes to so many doors nowadays just had pups in the kitchen. I sold them. Here's the money."

We live in a world of unending financial pressure. Christians experience all the financial demands of the world plus the multitude of financial needs of Christian ministries, missionaries, and churches. We could give away every dollar we have and still not satisfy all the requests that are made of us. What we need is a plan for financial stewardship. But in truth, Christian stewardship goes beyond how we allocate our financial resources. It encompasses everything we have: time, talent, and treasure since it all comes from God.

ASPECTS OF STEWARDSHIP

The word "steward" is primarily a New Testament word, referring to the manager of a household (either a slave or a freeman). The steward's duties could range from overseeing the care of the household's children to managing and allocating finances to overseeing other servants.

In Genesis 24, we meet Abraham's steward (Genesis 15:2, "steward" in KJV, "heir of my house" in NKJV), Eliezer of Damascus, who was to play an important role in Abraham's affairs. Eliezer was assigned the task of finding a wife suitable for Abraham's son, Isaac (verses 3–4). This single illustration shows just how much responsibility a trusted steward was given in the ancient world.

Accountability

Eliezer "ruled over all [Abraham] had" (verse 2); "all [Abraham's] goods were in his hand" (verse 10). Eliezer was obviously a trusted steward to have been given access to, and oversight of, all of Abraham's substantial resources and property.

Availability

There was no task outside the steward's realm of responsibility. In this case, taking a camel caravan to a distant land over several weeks' time was not too much to ask. The steward was available for whatever his master required.

Anxiousness

It's obvious from Eliezer's response to Abraham that he was anxious to do his job and do it well. He dialogued with Abraham about the details of the journey. He wanted to succeed for his master and accomplish the mission on which he was being sent. Eliezer's dialogue with his master is a precursor of the dialogue in prayer we have with God when we are intent on carrying out His will.

Allegiance

Eliezer took an oath by placing his hand "under the thigh of Abraham his master, and swore to him concerning this matter" (verse 9). Eliezer was committed to Abraham before taking this oath, so why was the oath necessary? Because it was a reaffirmation—a visible, timely statement of continuing commitment and allegiance. Today when I hear Christians say they don't want to sign a "commitment card" in a financial campaign of some sort, I wonder about their true commitment. There should be no hesitancy to provide tangible evidence of our continuing allegiance.

Agreeableness

Verses 12–14 record Eliezer's prayer to God for success in carrying out Abraham's will. We find nothing but agreeableness in all of Eliezer's attitudes toward his service to Abraham. So committed is he to doing a good job in administering Abraham's will that he prays to God for success—that God would show kindness to his master Abraham by granting him (Eliezer) success on his journey.

Attributing Praise

In verse 35 of Genesis 24, Eliezer is meeting the family of the bride-to-be for Isaac, and he extols Abraham before them—how the Lord has blessed his master. Eliezer's praise of Abraham is an indication that he finds great pleasure in being the steward of such a man. You can tell a lot about a master/owner by the way his stewards/employees talk about him when he is not around. This doesn't mean Abraham was perfect, but it does mean that Eliezer was a loyal steward, building up his master in the eyes of others.

CONCEPTS OF STEWARDSHIP

So, in summary, based on Elizer's characteristics, we can say that a steward is someone who, out of loyalty and commitment to his master, manages the master's affairs in the same way the manager would if he was managing them himself. The steward becomes an extension of the master, taking on the mind of the master and submitting his own will and preferences to those of the master. When he is required to act without specific input from the master, he uses his knowledge of the master's desires and past choices to make a decision.

Laban (Genesis 29–30) and Joseph (Genesis 39) provide further illustration of what it means to be a faithful manager of another's resources. Joseph ultimately became second in command over all of Egypt as a result of his faithfulness as a steward. He started out as the steward of Potiphar, one of Pharaoh's officials, and was put in charge of all of Potiphar's possessions and affairs. Genesis 39:6 says Potiphar eventually only showed up to eat his meals, leaving everything else to Joseph!

When Potiphar's wife tried to seduce Joseph sexually, he refused on the basis of his loyalty to Potiphar. He knew that Potiphar had entrusted everything to him, and what an act of disloyalty it would be if he violated that trust. Joseph was an amazingly loyal steward, and he was eventually blessed because of it .

Moving to the New Testament, we find two Greek words that can refer to stewards, and Galatians 4:2 contains both words: "but [he] is under guardians and stewards until the time appointed by the father." "Guardians" refers to someone who acted as a tutor (manager) for children, and a steward was someone who managed the whole household. In both cases the concept is the same—managing in the place of another, whether parents or owners.

Jesus used the idea of stewardship in His parables. In Matthew 20:8 a steward was instructed by the owner of a vineyard to gather the workers and pay them their wages. The same concept is found in Matthew 21, 25 and Luke 12, 19.

In Titus 1:7, Paul wrote that "a bishop must be blameless, as a steward of God." That means pastors and elders are acting as shepherds over something that belongs totally to God, not to them. The church, the people, the influence, the rewards—all of it belongs to God. Church leaders are nothing more than stewards.

Stewardship is more than just going to church and giving God ten percent of your income. Being a steward of God means that everything you have belongs to Him. Stewardship is an acknowledgement of that fact. Someday we will give an account to God for how we have used everything He entrusted to us.

PRINCIPLES OF STEWARDSHIP

Following are four principles that can be applied to any area of stewardship for the Lord.

God Owns Everything

The first principle is foundational to all the rest: God owns everything. A good way to realize how much we need this principle is to think of how often we use the phrase "my" in our daily conversations: "my car," "my job," "my money," "my time," "my family." We would be much more biblically accurate if we substituted the word "God's" for "my." I'm not suggesting we should—but I am suggesting that we should remember that it is He who owns everything and we who own nothing. The Bible is pretty clear about who owns everything: The land is God's (Leviticus 25:23), the earth

(Psalm 24:1), the beasts of the field (Psalm 50:10), the silver and gold (Haggai 2:8), every soul (Ezekiel 18:4), we ourselves (Romans 14:8).

We agonize over the possibility of "losing everything." How can we lose something that is not ours to begin with? If Christians would get this issue of ownership settled, it would take a lot of pressure off of the possibility of their losing it all. If it belongs to God, it is totally up to Him as to whether it remains in our hands or not.

We Are God's Administrators

The Bible is clear that it is God who provides wealth to us. "Every good gift and every perfect gift" is from Him (James 1:17); He is the one who gives the ability to accumulate wealth (Deuteronomy 8:18). We have created this notion in our culture of being a "self-made man," but nothing could be further from the truth. Yes, there is hard work and initiative; but more than anything, there is the blessing and provision of God. Even our creativity and strength to work comes from Him.

After giving great amounts of his personal wealth for the building of the first temple in Jerusalem, king David declared in 1 Chronicles 29:14, "For all things come from You, and of Your own we have given You." That is the essence of an understanding of stewardship: God gives to us; and from what He has given, we give back to Him. When we write a check and take it to church, we are not giving to God from our own but from His own.

The founder of Methodism, John Wesley, understood this principle wholly: "When the possessor of heaven and earth brought you into being and placed you in this world, He placed you here not as an owner, but as a steward; and as such, He entrusted you for a season with goods of various kinds. But the sole [ownership] of these still rests in Him. As you are not your own, but His, so is everything that pertaineth to you."

How We Administer Determines
How God Distributes

The third principle is this: Our stewardship of what God has given to us in the past determines what He will distribute to us in the future.

Historically, churches that emphasize tithing and giving regularly to the Lord have said "it's impossible to 'outgive' God"— and it is. But the idea was that whatever we gave to God, He was obligated to give more in return. That idea is far too mechanical to suit me. It leaves out the dynamic of our interest in God's work and exactly why we are giving the money to Him.

A better way to view our stewardship, and God's response to it, is to think of God as an owner/manager and we as His managers or stewards. He gives us a certain amount of His possessions to manage; and when we do a faithful job with what He has given, He gives more. When He sees that we have His interests in mind regarding how we use what He has provided, He naturally gives us more to manage. God does not give us His possessions to manage according to our goals and desires but according to His.

Matthew 25:21 captures this idea beautifully: "His lord said to him, 'Well done, good and faithful servant; you were faithful over a few things, I will make you ruler over many things. Enter into the joy of your lord'" (see also Luke 16:10–11). Many Christians make the mistake of thinking that when they have been made "ruler over many things," they will start to return a portion to God. No, they likely will not. It is what we do with small things that is the best indicator of what we will do with large things. The principle is to start small in faithfulness and see how God responds with more.

We Shall All Give an Account Someday

The last principle is one that should motivate us toward faithful stewardship: We will be called to give an account of our stewardship. Romans 14:12 says, "So then each of us shall give account of himself to God." For Christians, that accounting (note the use of the "financial" term) will take place at the judgment seat of Christ (2 Corinthians 5:10). It is not an accounting in terms of whether we have earned eternal life, but how faithful we have been as stewards of all God has given us in Christ. An easy way to think of what we have been given is in terms of time (we have all been given the same amount daily), talent (the gifts and abilities God has given each one), and treasure (the material resources we have). All of each category that we have has come to us as a gift from God and is to be managed ("stewarded") for His glory.

The great preacher John Broadus shocked his congregation one Sunday by walking up and down the aisles of his church with the ushers as the offerings were collected, watching what each person contributed. When he returned to the pulpit, he asked the congregation to consider their consternation at his seeing the small amounts they gave, when they were more than willing for God to see it each week. Somehow we don't think God sees and knows how faithful we are, or aren't—but He does!

I have not, and will not, do that as a pastor. But I will take Broadus' exhortation and deliver it to you: God is aware of what we do with what He has given. It is our job to be faithful stewards, for we will one day give an account of all.

As you work through this study guide on giving to God, may your heart be open to what God is saying to you about what you should do with what you have been given.

APPLICATION

1. In Titus 1:7 Paul calls a bishop a "steward of God." Explain how each of the characteristics in verses 7–9 relate to stewardship:

   a. Whose *will* does a steward carry out?

   b. Why should a steward of God not be *quick-tempered*?

   c. How would being addicted to *wine* be inconsistent with a steward of God?

   d. Why should God's stewards not be *violent*?

   e. How should a steward of God view *money*?

f. How should a steward use his *home*?

g. Why should *goodness* be found in a steward of God?

h. Why would not being *sober minded* be a fault?

i. What conflict would being *unjust* create?

j. Why should a steward be able to *control himself*?

k. Why should a steward of God be committed to *Scripture*?

l. In short, how do these characteristics represent God himself? Who is a steward of God supposed to be like?

2. To what aspect of the Christian life does Peter apply the concept of stewardship in 1 Peter 4:10?

  a. Why is one's spiritual gift similar to money as a matter of stewardship?

  b. What does God expect you to do with your spiritual gift?

c. When all the spiritual gifts given throughout the church are functioning, who does the church act like? Who is the world supposed to see when it sees the church in action?

d. Who does the world see (when it looks at the church) if Christians are not being good stewards of their spiritual gifts?

3. Read 1 Corinthians 4:1–2.

a. What did Paul say he was a steward of as an apostle of Christ? (verse 1)

b. What was the mystery of which he spoke? (Ephesians 3:1–12)

c. As a Christian commissioned to spread the Gospel, how do you also become a steward of those same mysteries?

d. What does Paul say is the chief requirement of any steward? (verse 2)

e. How does that apply to one who is a steward of the mysteries of God?

f. How is the Great Commission (Matthew 28:18–20) a "stewardship commission" in terms of the church doing what Jesus did?

4. Evaluate your own stewardship in terms of the following three areas:

a. Your time. To what degree are you conscious of using your time in a way that pleases God?

b. Your talent: How are you using your spiritual gift(s) and natural abilities for God's glory?

c. Your treasure: How do you demonstrate your stewardship when it comes to money?

DID YOU KNOW?

Scholars are not totally agreed upon the significance of Abraham having Eliezer make an oath while placing his (Eliezer's) hand under Abraham's thigh. The Hebrew word for thigh (*yarek*) referred to the region close to the loins and was used to refer to one's descendants (Genesis 46:26; Exodus 1:5; Judges 8:30). Since Eliezer's mission to find a wife for Isaac was critical to the covenant promises of God to Abraham of having many descendants, Abraham may have had Eliezer swear with his hand under his thigh as a way of impressing upon Eliezer that his mission was covenant-centric in terms of descendants.

THE SERMON ON THE AMOUNT

Malachi 3:10–14

In this lesson we will study the practice and priority of tithing for God's people.

OUTLINE

Christians in America have been found to give at about the same proportion as the population at large, and in a similar manner: incidentally and impulsively. Tithing, however, represents a method of giving filled with purpose, reflecting one's understanding of what God has done.

   I. **Tithing Was the Method of God**

  II. **Tithing Was a Matter of Priority with God**

 III. **Tithing Was a Means of Proving God**

 IV. **Tithing Was a Means of Provision by God**

  V. **Putting the Tithing Principle to Work**

When I came out of seminary and began to preach the Word of God, the first time I prepared to preach on the subject of money, I was extremely nervous. Somehow I had the idea that preaching on financial matters was not wise. But I soon changed my mind about that and have been preaching confidently and faithfully about money ever since.

Why? Because I quickly learned that God has much to say about money in His Word; and if I am going to declare the whole counsel of God, I am going to say what God says about money. In addition, I realized that not to preach on finances would be to rob Christians of the blessing that comes from living obediently to that particular part of the Bible.

No institution or organization is exempt from the catastrophes that can follow financial mismanagement, and that includes the church. Governments, businesses, churches, marriages—everywhere people and money mix, there is the possibility for failure. And so the church has to understand clearly the way God intended for His work on earth to be financed and managed. Fortunately, as I discovered in my own preaching ministry, the Word of God is full of guidelines about giving. And it is also clear about the blessings that come to those who manage their finances according to God's plan, including the church. It pains me to see churches resort to worldly methods for raising money while ignoring God's statutes and missing His blessings.

The guideline we will study in this lesson is found in Malachi 3:10–14. We are not Jews living in the Old Testament, but we find in this passage a principle and a promise concerning managing money. I have heard some Christians complain about drawing a principle for giving from the Old Testament, and just as often have discovered that their objection had more to do with giving a tithe of their income than the fact that the principle was found in the Old Testament.

As we will see, the tithe is not a Jewish or Christian principle, but a human principle: A tenth of everything belongs to God.

TITHING WAS THE METHOD OF GOD

For fifteen centuries, from Moses to Christ, the law of the tithe was in place in Israel. Whenever Israel disobeyed God's laws, she found herself being disciplined. The book of Malachi finds Israel having returned from a seventy-year period of discipline in Babylon.

The Jews are back in the land and Malachi is bringing them the Word of the Lord. Though they have just returned from captivity, the nation soon began to backslide and return to disobedient ways— including ignoring God's law of the tithe.

The principle of tithing (giving ten percent of one's income or possessions) is found in the Old Testament before it was codified in the Law of Moses. In Genesis 14, we find Abraham encountering Melchizedek, the king-priest of Salem. Abraham was returning from victory over a coalition of kings and gave Melchizedek a tithe of the war plunder (verse 20).

In Genesis 28:22 we find Jacob making a promise to pay a tithe to God if God would fulfill Jacob's requests. Now that is not an appropriate model for how to tithe, but it does show that the tithe was well-understood as a principle before the time of Moses and the Law.

Once we get to the Law of Moses under which Israel lived, we find that the tithe was more than just giving ten percent to God. There were, in fact, three different tithes. The first we can call "the Lord's tithe," and read about it in Leviticus 27:30–32: "And concerning the tithe of the herd or the flock, or whatever passes under the rod, the tenth one shall be holy to the Lord" (verse 32). This tithe can be generally compared to the taxes we pay as citizens of the United States. Israel was a theocracy (unlike the United States), so religious and civil aspects were combined. The tithe, in addition to being partially consumed in sacrifices, went to support the infrastructure of the government.

The second tithe was the Levites' tithe. Since the Levites (priests) had no inheritance of land in the Promised Land, they depended on the rest of the nation for support. The Levites' tithe consisted of foodstuffs grown on the land that were given for the support of the priests in the nation.

The third tithe occurred once every three years. Every third year every Israelite was to give a tithe of that year's income as a kind of charity tithe—to provide for widows, orphans, strangers, and others who had no means of support (Deuteronomy 14:22–29). Just as many churches today have benevolence funds for the poor or those otherwise in need, so this third tithe served that purpose in Israel. If this every-three-year tithe was averaged for each year, it would represent a three-and-one-third percent payment.

So the total annual tithe for the Israelite was ten percent plus ten percent plus three-and-one-third percent—or 23.3 percent annually.

But in addition to the tithes, the people also gave offerings to God. We find Malachi speaking for God to the post-captivity nation, that they had robbed God of His "tithes and offerings" (Malachi 3:8). There were many different kinds of offerings mentioned in the Old Testament. These offerings, combined with the 23.3 percent annual tithe, might have consumed as much as 40 percent of an Israelite's annual income.

So God had a plan—and it was for His people to faithfully support His work through tithes and offerings.

TITHING WAS A MATTER OF PRIORITY WITH GOD

The Israelites Malachi addressed had degenerated significantly since returning from captivity, spiritually speaking. In Malachi 1:8 he points out that when they brought an animal as a sacrifice to the Lord, instead of bringing the best of the flock, they would bring the worst—a weak, sick, or blind animal. Malachi says (paraphrase), "Offer such an animal to a human governor and he would never accept it. Yet you bring it as an offering to God!" A comparison would be if we gave to our civil government the same amount of taxes that the average Christian gives to God (one to three percent of income). The government would not accept that, yet we expect God to accept it.

Malachi says cursed are those who give to God the leftovers from their flock as a tithe or offering (Malachi 1:14). What is the world supposed to think about a God whose followers bring Him their worst instead of their best?

There's a fine line between doing the work of the Lord with excellence and trying to put on a show, and we have to be careful not to cross it. I encourage our church to give God our very best, whether it's in music or teaching or nursery work or missions— but not to try to outdo others or "be the best" for the sake of showing off. We never want to do that. But we do want to give God our best. He is a great God, a great King, and a great Lord and Savior, and He deserves the best we have to offer.

It takes work and sacrifice to offer God our best. We have to give up some things we might buy with the money we give to God. We have to give up time to come to choir and orchestra practice, or to take classes in being an excellent teacher. It costs us something to give God our best. I don't believe God is pleased when we take what's left at the end of the day or the end of the month and give it to Him.

The question for every Christian to ask is, "Am I giving God the first part of everything? My money when I get paid? My day when I arise in the morning? My time when called on to serve?" Or are we giving God only that which is left over after we have spent the first part on ourselves?

TITHING WAS A MEANS OF PROVING GOD

It sounds strange to us to think of God wanting to prove himself to man—more often, we think of trying to prove ourselves to Him. But in this matter of tithing, God was eager to prove himself to the nation of Israel. In Malachi 3:10, He tells the nation, "And try Me now in this [matter of tithing and see] if I will not open for you the windows of heaven and pour out for you such a blessing that there will not be room enough to receive it."

It must be stated that God was not selling His blessing for 10 percent of Israel's possessions. We saw Jacob trying to deal with God in Genesis 28, which was consistent with his conniving personality. But God doesn't deal with men in that fashion, though it has long been man's idea that he could buy the favor of God with money or good works. The Protestant Reformation was fueled by Martin Luther's sixteenth-century response to the idea that the church could sell favors from God. The church raised money by teaching that men could buy forgiveness for their sins. In effect, they were paying for the privilege of sinning without consequence. John Tetzel, one of the most well-known for this heresy, promoted it with this piece of verse: "Soon as the money in the coffer rings, a soul from purgatory springs."

But God is not for sale, and He wasn't offering His blessings to the Israelites in return for their tithe. Instead, the tithe represented obedience, and obedience represented faith. It was faithful obedience that would be rewarded, whether the obedience was in the form of the tithe or any other of God's laws.

Israel had just returned from seventy years in captivity in Babylon as a result of not being faithful to God. He was now offering the new generation of returning Israelites the opportunity to learn the lesson their fathers had ignored: God always honors and blesses faithful obedience. Tithing would be just one way the nation could put themselves on the road to blessing once again.

Tithing Was a Means of Provision by God

My wife and I, since the early days of our marriage, have used the tithe as the foundation of our financial stewardship. That doesn't mean we never had financial challenges, but it does mean that God has honored His Word and proven himself faithful to us through the years. It has been a decades-long adventure to see how God has met our needs over and over again.

I believe that is what God wanted to communicate to the Israelites: Trust Me and try Me and see if I will not provide for you. This is the way He put it to them in Malachi 3:11: "And I will rebuke the devourer for your sakes, so that he will not destroy the fruit of your ground, nor shall the vine fail to bear fruit for you in the field . . . ." God cares for us personally and promises to provide for those who are faithfully obedient to Him.

By "the devourer," God was saying that not only would He provide, He would protect. He would keep the enemies of Israel, both human and spiritual, from coming in and destroying what they had. I can recall many times when my wife and I drove cars and used appliances that, by all rights, should have long since stopped working. But I believe God stepped in and continued to meet our needs. And I believe that's what He does in His dual ministry of providing and protecting.

I have heard innumerable testimonies through the years of how God made a lot out of a little, helping families make it through times of financial shortage. It is a definite step and statement of faith to write a check to God at the beginning of the month and believe that God will not allow the month to outlast the remaining money. Too many Christians choose to pay and spend first, then give to God if they have anything left at the end of the month. That is not how tithing should work, nor is it a way to see God honor His promise to provide. One of the great surprises for people who begin to tithe is to see how God arranges the affairs of their lives to allow them to accomplish the same things they had accomplished before tithing, only now by spending ten percent less money.

Putting the Tithing Principle to Work

Many Christians object to the practice of tithing because it is based on law in the Old Testament, and in the New Testament we are supposed to live by grace. Is this a conflict? I like to ask such objectors whether they can think of any area of practice in which Jesus Christ lowered the requirements of a piece of Old Testament legislation for His followers. I'm not talking about the civil or ceremonial practices such as sacrifices and worship in the temple, but the moral and spiritual practices. I can't think of a single place where life under grace is to be any different spiritually than life under the Law. In fact, Jesus continually raised the plane higher as illustrated by His teachings in the Sermon on the Mount. Six times in Matthew 5, Jesus compared what the Jews had been taught in the Old Testament with His elevation of the same teaching. For instance, the Old Testament prohibited adultery, but Jesus said adultery was a matter of the heart and eyes, not just the body (Matthew 5:27–30).

For that reason, it is difficult for me to conceive that followers of Christ have been somehow released from the principle of tithing. If we consider tithing in the same category with the Matthew 5 teachings, we should be giving more than a tithe! We should be elevating giving to a higher plane than in the Old Testament.

The general principle in the New Testament is that we are to give as God prospers us (1 Corinthians 16:2). And just as in the Old Testament, we are to give, trusting that God will supply all our needs in Christ Jesus (Philippians 4:19). In the New Testament, an amount to give is never specified. Rather, giving is to be an expression of thanks to God for His bountiful grace. And since the tithe is never repudiated in the New Testament, I believe that is a good place to begin with giving.

Let me conclude by asking you to consider all the ways you demonstrate your beliefs with your money: education, adequate housing, reliable transportation, respectable clothing, and so on. To what degree is your giving to God a reflection of your belief in Him? If He is our highest commitment in life, should our giving not reflect that priority? God asks you to try Him and see if He will not honor your commitment.

1. From how many different sources was the Israelite required to tithe each year? (Deuteronomy 14:22–23)

   a. What was the purpose of the tithe? (verse 23)

   b. What application might be made to today? From how many sources of income should the Christian tithe?

   c. If God is the giver of all "income" regardless of its source, how does this argue for tithing from all our sources of income?

   d. How would you respond to the question that is often asked as to whether a Christian should tithe on gross or net income?

2. Read Numbers 18:25–32.

   a. To whom did the Israelites give a tenth of their "inheritance" (the produce from the land)? (verse 26a)

b. And what were the Levites to do with the tithe they received? (verses 26b, 28)

c. What were the Levites allowed to do with the remaining 90 percent? (verse 31)

d. What standard was used in selecting the portions for the tithe? (verse 29)

e. How do you apply this standard in terms of giving financially to the Lord? Do you give the Lord the first (the best) of your income or the last?

3. Read Deuteronomy 26:12–19.

a. What was the Israelite required to do after giving the third-year tithe? (verses 13–14)

b. Why were the people required to make this confession before God? (verses 15–17)

c. How did their obedience and integrity seal Israel's and God's mutual commitment? (verses 17–19)

d. How was their mutual generosity a sign of their mutual values?

e. What does it say when a Christian receives generously from God but does not reciprocate in generosity toward God and others?

4. From Matthew 5:21–48, list the six areas in which Jesus elevated the standards from the Old Testament to the New:

a. Verses 21–26

b. Verses 27–30

c. Verses 31–32

d. Verses 33–37

e. Verses 38–42

f. Verses 43–48

5. For what did Jesus chastise the Pharisees in Matthew 23:23?

a. Did He say anything about omitting the practice of tithing?

b. How does tithing compare to justice, mercy, and faith?

c. What does the last phrase of the verse suggest about continuing the practice of tithing?

6. To whom did Paul make the promise in Philippians 4:19?

   a. What motivated him to make such a promise? What had the Philippians done? (verses 10–18)

   b. In context then, to whom does the promise of God's provision apply?

DID YOU KNOW?

Israel was not unique in her practice of the tithe. Evidence of tithing has been found in discoveries and records pertaining to Egypt, Syria, Lydia, Babylon, Assyria, Ugarit, and Carthage. However, no other country appears to have established legislation as detailed as Israel's concerning the tithe. (From the *International Standard Bible Encyclopedia*.) The widespread practice of the tithe points to a universal truth of God that spread throughout the human population from its earliest introduction. Other such ancient truths, such as the flood described in Genesis, are also found in the histories of other nations. Universal practices point to universal truths established by God.

JESUS AT THE TREASURY

Mark 12:41–44

In this lesson we discover what matters most in our giving.

OUTLINE

Studies have shown that, in general, the more money people make, the smaller the percentage they give away. The dollar amounts increase, but the percent decreases. Jesus made the point that giving out of our surplus is not as important as giving out of our livelihood.

I. **The Affluence from Which We Give**

II. **The Amount That We Give**

III. **The Appraisal of What We Give**

IV. **The Lesson for What We Give**

OVERVIEW

Alfred Nobel was a Swedish chemist who made his fortune by inventing dynamite and other powerful explosive materials that were bought by the major governments of the world and used to produce weapons. Alfred Nobel had a brother; and when the brother died, the newspaper mistakenly ran biographical facts about Alfred instead of the brother. When someone sent Alfred Nobel a copy of the obituary, he read it with amazement. The newspaper writer had described the brother (thinking he was the famous inventor instead of Alfred) as a man who had become rich by enabling people to kill one another in unprecedented numbers. He was so shaken with this public assessment of his life that he resolved to use his great fortune to reward achievements that benefited humanity instead of destroying it. As a result, the Nobel Prizes in physics, chemistry, medicine, literature, and peace were established.

Alfred Nobel was given a rare opportunity to learn how people viewed his life before he died and to make adjustments to change that perception. All of us would do well to consider what an objective observer might say about the life we are living now and the legacy we will leave behind. What changes might we make if we were given access to that assessment?

While we may never get that totally objective evaluation of our life on earth, that doesn't mean it doesn't exist. God in heaven is watching our life moment by moment. He sees what we are doing and how we are living, and we will receive that evaluation (if we are a Christian) at the judgment seat of Christ (2 Corinthians 5:10).

Most of the time when we think of God watching our life, it is for the purpose of encouragement, protection, and provision. And He indeed does that. But how do you think our life will be evaluated at the judgment seat if He is not also watching in an evaluative way? In the passage of Scripture we will study in this lesson (Mark 12:41–44), we find an excellent example of God watching and evaluating the life of a person on earth.

Jesus spent the last day of His public ministry at the temple—Tuesday of Passion Week. In Herod's temple there were thirteen "treasuries" (receptacles) where people deposited coins. Each was shaped differently with a letter of the Hebrew alphabet corresponding to a word that described the purpose of each particular treasury. The treasuries had metal, trumpet-like openings into which coins were deposited and through which they rattled until they landed in a collection box below. Some people made a great show of bringing large amounts of small copper coins and throwing them in all at once so the resulting noise could be heard by all who were nearby. (This would be like us throwing in 100 pennies rather than just dropping in a dollar bill.) These people gave so they could be noticed and admired by others.

Jesus was sitting with His disciples, watching people put money into the treasuries. I find it interesting to note how much attention Jesus gave to matters of financial stewardship. Half of His parables, and fifteen percent of His teachings, were directed toward steward-ship. His attention was given to this subject because money is a mirror of life. We exert energy to work, and it gets transformed into money which we exchange for wants and needs. Even the smallest coin represents a part of who we are.

Faithful Old Testament saints would not have dreamed of com-ing into the temple empty-handed. For them, the essence of worship was returning to God a portion of what He had given to them. And so the temple in Herod's day had these thirteen treasuries estab-lished for Old Testament saints to make monetary offerings. (Nine were for required offerings and four were for free-will offerings.)

Verse 41 tells us that Jesus purposely "sat opposite the treasury and saw how the people put money into the treasury." He was close enough to see what a poor widow had in her hand when she came to deposit her offerings—two small copper coins. And He used what He saw to create an object lesson for His disciples about the nature of giving.

An unspoken lesson from this instance is that what we do with our money is God's business. He makes no apology for watching what the people were doing who approached the treasury. It's none of our business how other people spend their money because it's not our money they're spending. But because it's God's money, it is His business. I don't know what anybody in our church gives to the Lord, nor do I want to know. But I do want them to know that God knows and cares.

The question we need to consider, and which we can answer from this passage of Scripture, is, "What does God look for when He watches the treasury?"

THE AFFLUENCE FROM WHICH WE GIVE

One thing Jesus noted that day was the affluence from which people gave to the treasury. There were rich people who came and then there was the "one poor widow." When the New Testament describes her as poor, it doesn't mean just "not well-off." Instead, Mark used a Greek word that means one who crouches down, or cowers. Therefore, she was a self-conscious woman who lived in the crouched, cowering position of a pauper or beggar. She was a desperately poor woman—a widow with no husband to support her.

The point is that Jesus knows what we have. He knows if we have much or if we have nothing. In the church today, that poor widow would no doubt be told by more than one well-meaning Christian that God wouldn't expect her to give anything since she had so little. There are many Christians today who have little, relatively speaking—teenagers, college students, even some families—and they use their lack of abundance as a reason not to give to the Lord. But this poor widow did not hide behind her poverty. She gave what she could because she knew that God knew what she had.

THE AMOUNT THAT WE GIVE

Not only does God see the affluence out of which we give but He also sees the amount we give. He saw that the widow put in "two mites," which equaled a "quadran." A mite (Greek *lepton*) represented $\frac{1}{128}$th of a days' pay which was a denarius. She brought two mites to put into the treasury.

Over a lifetime, most people will see a staggering amount of money pass through their hands. Even if it seems like a small amount when we bring home our paycheck, over a lifetime it represents a lot—far more than the poor widow had. Our holding back from the Lord because we don't have very much is not going to be seen as valid when we look at our income over a lifetime. On the basis of Jesus' observation of the widow, God does see how much we give in spite of what we don't have.

The widow Jesus observed only had two mites to her name: "she . . . put in all that she had, her whole livelihood." So the idea that just because we have little means we can't give to the Lord is not valid. This woman had little and gave it all. Jesus referred to what she gave as "her whole livelihood." It's not hard to figure out why He used her as an example.

The question for us is, What part of our livelihood does our giving represent? If the whole world knew what I give, would I want them to know? The more important question is, Since God does know how my giving measures against my livelihood, am I happy with what He knows? Does my gift represent me? Am I happy to be represented before God by my gift?

THE APPRAISAL OF WHAT WE GIVE

We are highly offended by the thought that any person might pass judgment on what we give. But without apology, God does pass judgment; and we need to allow His appraisal to impact our giving appropriately.

The first thing we have to understand is that God's math is different than ours. It would have to be for Jesus to say that a woman who gave $2/128\text{ths}$ of a day's wage gave more than the rich people who gave multiple times more. In fact, Jesus appears to say that she gave "more than all those who have given to the treasury" combined (verse 43).

Here is one way to justify what Jesus said: Because of the way this widow's example has served to change many peoples' giving practices over the last 2,000 years, Jesus might have been looking down through time and saying, "By this woman's sacrificial gift, huge amounts of money have been returned to the Lord following her example, whereas no one was motivated to give more by a rich person who gave out of his abundance." Every time the story is told of the poor widow who gave all she had, someone is moved to give more sacrificially to God. In that sense, what the widow gave that day far exceeded what all the rich people gave that day. Her gift has been compounded over the last two centuries like no other act of financial giving in history.

More literally, focused on what she gave that day, Jesus said she gave more because she gave out of her poverty whereas the others gave out of their abundance. A more literal reading of the text would be that "they gave out of their surplus, she gave out of her life." What they gave had no impact on their life, but what she gave touched the very core of her survival.

The bottom line of God's appraisal is that He doesn't evaluate our giving by what we give as much as by what we have (2 Corinthians 8:12). A study was done a few years ago on patterns of giving in the United States. Those who gave the largest percentage of their income made $10,000 or less each year. Those who made between $10,000 and $20,000 gave a smaller percentage. The percentage dropped with each incremental stage of increased income. Those making $100,000 gave the smallest percentage of all. The amount was greater but the percentage was smaller.

It's amazing how poor, humble people are blessed by God; and then when they prosper, they forget about God. Some have wondered why God is still blessing America with great wealth when we have departed from our godly heritage. And the reason may be that our great wealth may be part of God's judgment rather than His blessing. A leader in the persecuted church in Romania wrote that 95 percent of the believers who face the test of persecution pass it, while 95 percent of those who face the test of prosperity fail it. Maybe that's what Thomas Carlisle was thinking when he said, "Adversity is hard on a man; but for one man who can stand prosperity, there are a hundred that can stand adversity." Far too often, the more we have, the less we give. And God sees it all.

THE LESSON FOR WHAT WE GIVE

An illustration from physics might help: The larger the mass, the greater the pull the mass exerts. That's why large planets are able to keep a large number of satellite moons orbiting around them. Apply that to wealth: The larger the total mass of our wealth, the greater pull it exerts on us; the harder it is for us to break away from its influence. Just as a smaller moon is defined in terms of the larger planet, so do we become defined in terms of our possessions.

God always uses contrasts in His Word to illustrate truth. Way back in the Old Testament, you have wealthy but generous Abraham contrasted with wealthy but self-centered Lot. One continued to be blessed, one did not. In the New Testament, we find generous Barnabas who sold his property and gave the proceeds to the church, contrasted with selfish Ananias and Sapphira who sold their property and kept some of the proceeds for themselves, lying to God and the apostles in the process. One continued to be blessed, the others died in their sins.

In the Gospels we find Mary with her alabaster flask of costly perfume which she used to minister to Jesus, contrasted with Judas, a thief who stole money from Jesus and the other disciples. Mary is remembered for her sacrifice, while Judas is re-membered in shame. And at the end of his life, a poor apostle named Paul was beheaded by a rich emperor named Nero. One lived for prosperity in heaven while the other sought prosperity on earth. Today we name our sons Paul and our dogs Nero.

The poor widow that Jesus used as an example gave her all to God because she believed that God would take care of her and meet her needs. I think many Christians today hold so tightly to what they have as much out of a lack of trust in God as out of a love of materialism. We trust God with our eternal soul, but have a harder time trusting Him for our daily bread.

A man told his pastor he wasn't giving to God because he had so many bills to pay every month. The pastor offered to pay whatever bills the man couldn't pay if he would begin putting God first and giving consistently. The man was amazed at such an offer but agreed. "Isn't it interesting that you'll trust me, a frail human being, to meet your needs but you won't trust God to do the same thing."

The final analysis of this snapshot out of the life of our Lord is that we have two people living for two different worlds. The woman saw past her own poverty and looked into eternity. The rich were living for this world and keeping plenty in hand to make sure that their status quo would not be interrupted. One person was moving away from her treasury toward God's while the other group of people was doing the opposite.

The irony is that the person whose treasure is in heaven is always moving toward his true treasure while moving away from his earthly treasure. That's why those who give generously to God have great cause for rejoicing. The widow woman, by giving to God, was essentially sending what she had to God, knowing that she would eventually catch up with it in heaven.

When we stand before God one day, there will be no opinions or partiality or any problem getting at the real truth of who we are. What God has seen in our lives will be fully revealed. The truth is, by looking into His Word, we can know today what God knows. And we can change our priorities and actions if we choose to do so.

1. In James 1:9, what does James say the poor man should do?

    a. What glory is there in being poor? (Luke 6:20)

    b. What does James say will happen to the rich? (verse 10)

    c. Is James talking about anyone who is rich? If not, what attitude of mind is he associating with the rich who will "fade away" in their pursuits?

2. What does James say is true of the poor in James 2:5?

    a. Are all poor people "rich in faith and heirs of the kingdom"? If not, what is James talking about? Why are the poor usually more receptive to the Gospel message?

b. How do the rich sometimes dishonor the poor? (verse 6;
see James 2:1–4)

c. How is God's name blasphemed when the poor are
dishonored? (verse 7)

d. Why did James condemn the unrighteous rich in James 5:1–6?
How were they mistreating the poor?

3. How did the early church in Jerusalem reach out to the poor
and meet their needs? (Acts 2:45; 4:32–37)

a. What experience have you had with poverty—either first-hand
or ministering to the poor—that follows this model?

b. What have you experienced about the generosity of the
poor? Why are the poor often more willing to share what
they have than are the rich?

4. Read Deuteronomy 8:10–20.

   a. What warning did Moses give the generation that was
      about to inherit the abundance of the Promised Land?
      (verses 10–11)

   b. What would they be tempted to think once they got settled
      in the land? (verses 12–14)

   c. What had God done for them that they would be tempted
      to forget? (verses 15–16)

   d. What is a sure sign of carnality when one begins to
      accumulate wealth? (verse 17)

e. What is the truth that the rich are wise to remember? (verse 18)

f. In general terms, what were the rich before they became wealthy?

g. If they were once poor themselves, why is it fitting that they behave generously toward the poor?

5. Read Luke 6:20–23 and Matthew 6:19–21.

   a. What is the general economic and spiritual condition of the people being described in Luke 6:20–22?

   b. Where is the reward of that group of people to be found? (verse 23)

c. The poor don't have a choice about where their treasure is. What about those who do have a choice? What did Jesus say to them in Matthew 6:19–21?

d. How does one go about storing up treasures in heaven?

DID YOU KNOW?

Mark mentions two units of money in his account of the woman at the treasury. The widow's "mite" (*lepton*) was a coin known to those living in Israel. But Mark also says the two mites represented a quadrans, a Latin (Roman) monetary unit (Greek *kodrantes*) that would have been familiar to those living in Rome who would have been unfamiliar with the *lepton*. Luke, the other gospel writer who records this event, does not mention the Roman quadrans since the recipients of his letter were Greek. The fact that Mark mentions the quadrans gives evidence that he wrote his gospel for readers in Rome.

DRAWING INTEREST

Selected Scriptures

In this lesson we study three biblical and spiritual principles of stewardship.

OUTLINE

Many Christians, even many pastors, don't believe sermons on money have a place in the church. But a study of the New Testament reveals that financial stewardship is no less spiritual a topic than the resurrection of Jesus Christ. Spiritual things happen when stewardship is practiced.

I. The Principle of Prior Consecration

II. The Principle of Proper Motivation

III. The Principle of Personal Responsibility

I n this lesson we are going to delve right into three principles of stewardship that can inform and guide our giving to the Lord. These are not my ideas, nor did I get these principles from a book on personal finances from the local bookstore. They are directly from the Word of God. As such, they are infallible principles that cannot be ignored; and when implemented, carry with them the blessing of God.

THE PRINCIPLE OF PRIOR CONSECRATION

The first principle is found in 2 Corinthians 8:5: "but they first gave themselves to the Lord, and then to us by the will of God." The principle found in this verse is that our giving of our resources is a reflection of having already given ourselves to God. When we say, "Lord, I give myself to You," that obviously includes the material resources we have. No one who has committed himself wholly to the Lord will have any hesitation in giving generously of his resources. And I believe the opposite is also true: Anyone who struggles with giving money to the Lord may not have consecrated himself wholly to the Lord.

Paul had asked the churches in Macedonia to help with a relief effort for the struggling church in Jerusalem. And the Macedonians responded generously by giving not only their money but themselves as well.

The principle of prior consecration recognizes that God is the owner of everything. He says in Ezekiel 18:4, "Behold, all souls are Mine." Every person in the world is God's, including what that person owns (see also Romans 14:8). First Corinthians 6:20 says, "For you were bought at a price; therefore glorify God in your body and in your spirit, which are God's." The principle of prior consecration simply recognizes that what the Bible says is true: God owns us and everything we possess, and using our possessions for His glory is the proper response to that fact. God's priority is on our relationship with Him, not our money. When our lives are consecrated to Him, giving is a natural outcome. To be sure, stewardship is a holy and spiritual endeavor, but it must be based in our spiritual relationship with God.

Giving is probably the most direct means of validating a person's spiritual claims. Some people may give lots of money away, even to

God, without having a relationship with Him. So giving is not an indicator of spiritual life. But for the person who has a relationship with Christ and is seeking to live for God, giving becomes a barometer of how fully their life is consecrated to God. A person's checkbook is a good indicator of how much of his heart is given over to God.

I have had Christians tell me that they have their spiritual life together except for the area of stewardship. Usually it's because they are waiting to "get ahead" financially, pay some bills, or reach a goal in their career. Once they get where they want to be financially, they'll start giving to the Lord. Usually, it never happens. They keep seeking to acquire just a little bit more and never reach the financial cushion that will allow them to have enough to give. Faithfulness to God has nothing to do with having enough. Our responsibility is to be faithful, to be consecrated, today. Only then will we enjoy the blessing of God on all our life.

I have learned something about the priority of stewardship that I was never taught in seminary: There is a direct connection between stewardship and spiritual revival and health in churches. Many churches are afraid to teach and preach about stewardship; but I believe those who do, prosper spiritually. I'm not sure I can explain that, but I have seen it too many times not to believe it's true. Whenever I preach on stewardship in my church—usually every January—interesting things happen. People make decisions for Christ in our services without a single salvation verse from Scripture being mentioned. People come forward to be baptized and to join the church without any word being spoken from the pulpit on those subjects. Somehow good things happen spiritually as a by-product of our being faithful in the area of stewardship.

If you are not practicing the principle of prior consecration in your life, I suggest you draw a circle on the ground and tell God, "Lord, everything in this circle belongs to You." Then step inside the circle.

THE PRINCIPLE OF PROPER MOTIVATION

Concerning one's motivation to give, I have often heard people say that those in the Old Testament had no choice—they lived under the law and were required to give; that they were dragged kicking and screaming to the temple with their offerings. There may have been some who gave that way in the Old Testament, just as there are probably some who give begrudgingly in the New Testament. In either case, God is vitally interested in the motivation of the believer.

The key verse for this second principle is 2 Corinthians 9:7: "So let each one give as he purposes in his heart, not grudgingly or of necessity; for God loves a cheerful giver." The Bible doesn't want us to give out of a burden of guilt but out of a grateful heart.

When I studied the Old Testament laws for giving, I discovered that the motivation for giving was the same as it is in the New Testament. Exodus 25:2 talks about an Israelite bringing offerings "willingly with his heart." First Chronicles 29:9 says, "Then the people rejoiced, for they had offered willingly, because with a loyal heart they had offered willingly to the Lord." Those verses sound exactly like 2 Corinthians 9:7. Read this version of Paul's words from the *Amplified Bible*. This sounds like the kind of giving we find in the Old Testament: "Let each one [give] as he has made up his own mind *and* purposed in his heart, not reluctantly or sorrowfully *or* under compulsion, for God loves (He takes pleasure in, prizes above other things, and is unwilling to abandon or to do without) a cheerful (joyous, 'prompt to do it') giver [whose heart is in his giving]."

That's the way giving is supposed to be done! We ought to be excited about the prospect of giving to God as an expression of our love and appreciation for Him, not resentful of losing something that we think belongs to us.

I heard a story once of a woman who dozed off during church. She woke up, still a bit groggy and confused, just when an usher was handing her a collection plate to start down her pew. Suddenly, in her foggy, half-awake and half-asleep state, instead of a collection plate she saw the nail-scarred hand of Christ. And instead of the face of an usher, she saw the thorn-scarred face of her Savior. And she never looked at giving the same way again. She stopped thinking of giving money to the church and began thinking of giving as an act of gratitude to the Savior who had bled and died for her.

When we consider that our giving is to Christ instead of to an organization, it will change forever the way we give. How could we not give willingly and with a glad heart to One who gave himself for us? If Jesus Christ walked into your church next Sunday morning with the scars of His brutal beating and crucifixion still visible in His body, I imagine the giving would be entirely different. But is He not there every Sunday? For those with eyes to see, He is.

People give grudgingly because they think they are giving to an organization run by men and women just like themselves, and they often don't agree with what those people are doing with "their" money. But when our focus is on giving to Jesus Christ, everything changes. When we give to Christ, whom we trust with our eternal life, we are giving to One who has given His all for us. And that changes everything.

THE PRINCIPLE OF PERSONAL RESPONSIBILITY

The third principle is that of personal responsibility, and we find it highlighted in 1 Corinthians 16. The most important thing to know about 1 Corinthians 16 is that it follows chapter 15, one of the most critical passages in the New Testament. First Corinthians 15 is the long chapter where Paul establishes the doctrine of the resurrection of believers based on the resurrection of Christ.

The resurrection of Christ sets Christianity apart from all the other religions of the world. We have a Savior who was not only crucified but who was brought back to life and lived on earth almost two months before ascending to heaven. First Corinthians 15 says that without the Resurrection, our faith is futile. The resurrection of Christ is absolutely essential to the Christian faith.

Paul's very last words in chapter 15—just before he begins discussing stewardship in chapter 16—are a bridge between the resurrection of Christ and Christian stewardship: "Therefore, my beloved brethren, be steadfast, immovable, always abounding in the work of the Lord, knowing that your labor is not in vain in the Lord." That is, because the sting of death has been removed by the Resurrection, we are to be immovable in the work of the Lord, fearing nothing.

It's important to remember that there were no chapter and verse divisions in Paul's original letters—they were added much later. Because we often stop reading at the end of a chapter, and pick up the next chapter later, we miss Paul's connection. He went from discussing the Resurrection to stewardship without missing a beat—from 15:58 to 16:1 without a pause. His transition from talking about the resurrection of Christ to taking up a monetary collection was seamless.

What does this say? For Paul, money was just as spiritual as was the resurrection of Jesus. That's not to say money is as important as the Resurrection, but it is to say that money is just as much a spiritual topic as the Resurrection. Those today who think money is not a spiritual topic need to learn from Paul that it most definitely is.

Paul's instruction in personal responsibility begins in 16:2, laying aside funds each week for the Lord in proportion to how the Lord has prospered you. God is not going to hold churches or Sunday school classes or Bible study groups responsible for their stewardship. Nor will He hold any individual responsible for the giving of another (a husband for a wife, or vice versa, for example). Giving is a *personal* matter. Each one will give account "of himself to God" (Romans 14:12; 2 Corinthians 5:10).

I've heard men say that, in their family where both the husband and wife work, they tithe from the husband's income but not from the wife's. I know there are many teenagers who work at part-time jobs who don't give to the Lord from their income, and many children who get allowances who don't set aside a portion for God. But every individual is responsible before God for giving to the Lord. It is a matter of personal, not corporate, responsibility.

The great English preacher Joseph Parker wrote these words on this subject: "One may search in vain throughout the entire New Testament for a single divine command or even entreaty addressed to the church as a whole. It is always the individual believer that is in view. It ought not be said, then, that the church is responsible to give to the Lord's work. To think in such a vein makes it all too easy for individual members when the annual church benevolent report is read to take smug satisfaction in the total amount expended by their church, though they themselves have scarcely contributed a penny. Unfortunately, Scripture gives no assurance that God reads the annual report."

Many Christians take great pride in how much their church gives to missions, social ministries, and outreaches of various sorts, even though they themselves give little or nothing to the church. But God's words about responsibility are never to churches corporately but to the individual members of churches. It is individuals, not churches, who will one day be held accountable for their giving.

Note the repetition of singular pronouns in the following verses on giving (italics added):

- Galatians 6:6 "Let *him* . . . share . . . ."
- 1 Corinthians 16:1–2 "On the first day of the week let *each one* of you . . . ."
- 2 Corinthians 9:6 "*He* who sows sparingly . . . *he* who sows bountifully . . . ."
- 2 Corinthians 9:7 "So let *each one* give as *he* purposes in *his* heart."

Those pronouns are not accidental. "Churches" and "organizations" are not addressed; individuals are. Dr. George W. Truitt, the eminent preacher whose pulpit was later filled by Dr. W. A. Criswell at First Baptist Church in Dallas, wrote these words: "When we turn to the New Testament, which is Christ's guide book and law for His people, we find that the supreme emphasis is everywhere placed upon the individual. The individual is segregated from the family. He is segregated from the church. He is segregated from the state and the society. He is segregated from his earthly friends or institutions, and he is brought into direct dealings with God himself. Everyone must give account of himself to God. There can be no sponsors or deputies or proxies in any such vital truth. Neither persons nor institutions, how ever dear and powerful, may dare to come between the individual and God."

These words, and the New Testament's emphasis on giving, are reflective of the New Testament doctrine of the priesthood of the believer. This means that every believer stands individually before God, accountable to Him for everything. We don't need a priest to represent us before God. Each Christian stands before God on his own and is thus accountable on his own.

I believe most churches are like the church I pastor—made up predominantly of middle-class, average-income folks. That means it takes every individual who has resources to be accountable to give of those resources to God. If every individual in every church in America would tithe of his or her income, there would be no lack of funds for ministry. In too many churches, the 80/20 rule holds: 20 percent of the people give 80 percent of the money.

People too often think that 10 percent of their relatively small income won't make any difference to a large church budget. But what if everyone in the church thought that way? When every individual fulfills his personal responsibility to give, God will supply all that every church needs.

Give yourself first to God. Give out of a willing and grateful heart. Fulfill your personal responsibility to give. These three spiritual principles of stewardship will change the spiritual life of every Christian who practices them.

1. Read 2 Corinthians 8:1–5.

   a. To what did Paul attribute the Macedonians' ability to give sacrificially to the needy Jerusalem church? (verse 1)

   b. What is there in verse 2 that suggests the grace of God was at work? That is, what was happening in the Macedonian churches that seemed beyond human ability?

   c. What two contrasting characteristics were present in the Macedonian churches at the same time? (verse 2)

   d. What is the difference in giving according to one's ability and giving beyond one's ability? (verse 3)

   e. What seems odd (according to modern practice) about who was doing the asking in this case—Paul or the Macedonians? (verse 4) Who usually does the asking today? What does this reversal suggest about how attitudes toward giving have changed?

f. In Greek, the word "fellowship" means "oneness" or "commonality." What does the use of this word in verse 4 suggest about how the Macedonians viewed their relationship to the saints in Jerusalem?

g. Why was the grace of God available to the Macedonians? (verse 5)

h. If the Macedonians had been carnal Christians, not fully given to the Lord, what do you think their response to the Jerusalem church would have been? According to their ability? Beyond their ability?

i. How many Christians do you know today who would deepen their own poverty to give to others who had even less?

2. What does Paul say in 2 Corinthians 8:12 is more important—willingness or the amount of the gift? In fact, how does willingness make any size gift acceptable to God?

a. When the Israelites were building the tabernacle, what was the sole condition for giving? (Exodus 25:2) What does that suggest about the acceptability of a gift if it was brought under pressure? How does this "invitation" to give differ from the kind of pressure sometimes exerted in modern invitations to give?

b. How did the Macedonians fulfill Moses' instructions about giving to the poor in terms of their attitude? (Deuteronomy 15:7–8, 10–11)

c. What attitude did David pray would always be found among the people of Israel? (1 Chronicles 29:17–18)

3. In Matthew 5:23–24 what order or priorities did Jesus establish concerning giving and having a clear conscience before God and one's neighbor?

    a. Which brings more pleasure to God—a gift or the reconciling of a relationship?

    b. How did Saul get these priorities—gifts versus obedience to God—out of order? (1 Samuel 15:22)

4. Rank the three principles in this lesson in terms of your own life (1 = most faithful, 3 = least faithful):

    1.

    2.

    3.

DID YOU KNOW?

Throughout the history of the development of the Hebrew Old Testament, evidence exists for the division of the text into small units, what we might refer to today as chapters and verses. The Old Testament chapter divisions we are familiar with today were added by the Anglican Stephen Langton, an archbishop of Canterbury (d. 1228) under the influence of the Latin Vulgate edition of the Bible. The New Testament's chapters and verses were added by a Parisian printer, Robert Stephens, in 1551. His edition of the Vulgate in 1555 was the first complete Bible with today's divisions, and the Geneva edition in 1560 was the first English version.

THE MEANING OF SACRIFICE

2 Corinthians 8

In this lesson we learn about the nature and necessity of sacrifice.

OUTLINE

Whether it's the freedoms we enjoy or the comfort of a padded pew on Sunday, it's easy to forget the price paid by those who sacrificed for us. Sacrifice is the midwife at the birth of everything good, great, and godly. For the Christian, sacrifice means making something sacred.

I. The Illustration of Sacrifice
   A. The Wealth That Was His
   B. The Poverty That Was His

II. The Necessity of Sacrifice

A few years ago, the Washington Post newspaper conducted interviews with a number of Hollywood personalities. They wanted to find out what made these celebrities tick—what they found interesting in life, what they lived for, and what they saw as the purpose of their life. One of the interviewees was the actress Shirley MacLaine, and here is the statement she made concerning her life's goals:

"The most pleasurable journey in life is through yourself. The only sustaining love involvement is with yourself. When you look back on your life and try to figure out where you've been and where you're going, when you look at your work, your love affairs, your marriages, your children, your pain and your happiness, when you examine all that closely, what you really find out is that the only person you really go to bed with is yourself. The only thing you have is working to the consummation of your own identity, and that's what I've been trying to do all of my life."

While that may sound unique to you, it is not unique to a large part of our modern society. Living for oneself seems to be a high priority for many people; looking out for "Numero uno," as they say. Like everything in our culture, this preoccupation with self has even made its way into the church. The more our culture devolves, the more my conscience is pierced as I contemplate the words of many of the church's great hymns: "Take my life and let it be, consecrated Lord to Thee"; "All to Jesus I surrender, all to Him I freely give"; "Have Thine own way, Lord, have Thine own way; Thou art the potter, I am the clay."

I have to ask myself whether I am living out the words of those hymns or whether I have allowed the world to squeeze me into its mold. Am I more concerned about God and His kingdom or about myself? Have I really surrendered all to Jesus or am I holding back much of what I have for myself? Have I lost touch with the biblical idea of sacrifice?

Unfortunately, we have lost touch with the older meaning of the word sacrifice. Today we think a sacrifice is to give up one thing in order to make something else happen. To use an extreme example, someone might say, "I sacrificed taking the cruise to the Bahamas in order to get my new diamond ring." That's really not what the word sacrifice means.

Our English word "sacrifice" comes from the Latin word *sacrificium*, itself made up of two Latin words: *sacer* (sacred) and *facere* (to make). Therefore, sacrifice literally means "to make sacred" or "to make holy," a meaning which has its roots in the Old Testament concept of sacrifice. When an Israelite went to his herd or flock to select an animal to offer as a sacrificial offering, the very act of choosing that animal was an act of making it holy. The animal didn't change, but the act of setting it aside for God made it holy. The animal no longer belonged to the person, it now belonged to God. Setting anything aside for God was to make it holy.

There are instances in the Gospels (still an Old Testament environment) of people making things holy. In Matthew 26 we find Mary of Bethany giving an expensive bottle of perfume to the Lord, anointing Jesus with it. In doing so, she sacrificed it—made it holy—to the Lord. The poor widow in Luke 21 put all she had to live on into the temple treasury. She took what she had and put it into God's hands. In doing so she made it holy—sacrificed it—to Him.

Also, in the days of the early church in Jerusalem, we read of members selling various things they owned in order to provide for members who were poor. In doing so, they took their property and set it aside for God's work—they sacrificed it to Him. Barnabas is the prime example we have of someone who did this, though there were others as well (Acts 4:34–37). And in the previous lesson, we mentioned the Macedonian Christians who went beyond their natural ability to give and gave sacrificially. That is, they took some of their meager funds and set them aside for their brethren in Jerusalem—they gave that money to God.

Some people refer to money as "filthy lucre," but that is a demeaning term. Money is amoral. It can be used for evil purposes, but it can also be made holy when it is given to God for His purposes. We are stewards of what God has given us, and it is up to us to determine how the money we have will be used. When we take something and give it totally back to God, we sacrifice it or make it holy. We remove it from the mundane, or profane, realm of this world and make it holy unto God.

THE ILLUSTRATION OF SACRIFICE

Paul uses the Lord Jesus Christ as the supreme example of one who gave up His wealth and became poor in order that we who were poor might become spiritually rich (2 Corinthians 8:9).

The Wealth That Was His

There are three dimensions to the sacrifice made by Jesus Christ for us.

1. He sacrificed the spiritual realm for the realm of humanity.

    It is impossible for us to imagine the change made by Jesus Christ when He left heaven and came to earth, left a purely spiritual domain and entered the physical realm of sinful humanity. He was spirit and not flesh. When He entered our realm, He took on the limitations of physical existence—being hungry, being tired, being limited to one place at a time. But He gave up His spiritual existence—sacrificed it to God—in order to come and dwell among us that we might gain a spiritual inheritance for eternity. A step down for Him, a step up for us.

2. He sacrificed the presence of God for the presence of men.

    Jesus was eternally present with God; but when He came to earth, He became present with men. In fact, He was given the name Immanuel which means "God with us" (Isaiah 7:14; Matthew 1:23). He was no longer God with God, but was God with man. He sacrificed that presence to come to earth.

3. He sacrificed the beauty of heaven for the streets of earth.

    Not only can we not imagine what it was like for Christ to have given up the spiritual realities of heaven to come to earth, neither can we imagine what it must have been like to give up the sheer beauty of heaven. We think our earth is a beautiful place, and indeed it is. But I do not believe it can compare with the beauty of heaven based on the glimpses of the New Jerusalem we have in the book of Revelation. Christ set the enjoyment of that beauty apart for God in order to do His will and come to earth.

The Poverty That Was His

That's what Christ set aside—sacrificed—for the Father. What He took upon himself, the poverty of humanity, was stunning in its contrast to what He sacrificed to come to earth.

1. He emptied himself.

    Paul wrote to the Philippians that Jesus emptied himself of His godly prerogatives and took upon himself the form of humanity. Based on the pictures artists have painted of Christ through the centuries, we sometimes get the impression that we would have immediately noticed Christ in His humanity had we passed Him on the street. But Scripture says otherwise (Isaiah 53:2). From his childhood on, Jesus looked as average as any other Jewish male in Israel. Even after He began His public ministry, it was only His teachings and miracles (and character) that distinguished Him from the crowd. In all other respects, His humanity was as average and normal as anyone else's. In other words, there was nothing "God-like" about Jesus the man. He emptied himself of all such distinguishing marks when He became a man.

2. He became a servant.

As a man, Jesus didn't try to become a leader in the worldly sense. He didn't engage in self-promotion. Instead, He did just the opposite of what, from the world's point of view, a king would do: He became a servant (Mark 10:45). Though the four gospels are filled with examples of Jesus' service to others, the definitive image of Him as a servant is when He washed the feet of His disciples (John 13).

3. He had nothing.

When Christ gave up heaven to come to earth, He gained nothing from earth in return. As He himself said, "Foxes have holes and birds of the air have nests, but the Son of Man has nowhere to lay His head" (Luke 9:58). He didn't own a home or property, had no regular income, and spent His life dependent on God's provision for His needs. He began His life in the most humble of circumstances, being born in a stable, and never rose above that standing during His years on earth. He was even buried in a borrowed tomb. Jesus sacrificed glory and gained poverty in return.

It's no wonder that Paul referred to Christ's coming to earth this way: "Great is the mystery of godliness: God was manifested in the flesh" (1 Timothy 3:16). Even Paul didn't fully understand the incarnation—what it meant for the Son of God to become the Son of Man and dwell on sin-sick planet earth.

We may not know all of what it was like for Him, but we do know what wealth became ours as a result of His sacrifice. Think of how different your life would be if Christ had not sacrificed heaven for you. Your sins are forgiven, you have the promise of an eternal home in heaven, you have the Spirit of God dwelling within, you have the opportunity to fellowship with others of like precious faith, you have the Word of God that contains principles by which you live your life with wisdom, leading to success in many areas; you have ready access to the throne of God for prayer, and you have a Savior and Lord who has promised to be with you always, even to the end of the age.

THE NECESSITY OF SACRIFICE

Nothing that is great or good or godly has ever happened in the history of man that was not born out of sacrifice. Mothers know this better than fathers—the pain and travail of childbirth is perhaps the greatest and most consistent reminder that there is a price to be paid for life.

Businessmen know this. Those who started with just an idea and invested their own blood, sweat, and tears to build a business know that nothing great comes without sacrifice. Churches and ministries know this as they pray and labor to bring something into existence that most of the world thinks is unnecessary. Sacrifice is at the heart of ministry.

Our forefathers knew this. It's easy, many generations later, to lose sight of the sacrifice made by our founding fathers, and then the waves of immigrants who came to this country seeking freedom and a new life, and then those of "the greatest generation" who defended the world against tyranny in the world wars.

But in truth, there are new sacrifices for every generation to make. There are always challenges and prices to pay personally: in our families, in our churches, and nationally. And never is that more true than in the financial realm. As long as some remain in the world who have not yet heard the Gospel and had the opportunity to know Christ, we are called to invest ourselves in that mission. We are called to set aside everything we have and all that we are, and make it holy—to dedicate it all to God for His glory and the accomplishment of His purposes. We will have all eternity to enjoy the fruits of that sacrifice. But until then, we are called to remember the necessity of sacrifice.

I visited not long ago a ministry to street people and the homeless in our community. It was started by a man who has given everything he owned to ministering to those who have no one else to turn to. He can take care of up to forty individuals in two large, rambling houses he bought. He and his family live there and minister to those who come to them for help. And gradually others are coming alongside to help support his work. But he started the ministry and continues to operate it sacrificially—because sacrifice is what we call setting aside all we have for the purposes of God.

I was not involved in the founding of the church I now pastor, but I know enough of its history to know it only happened sacrificially. When visitors look at our campus today and learn about the high school, college, and associated ministries, it's easy to think God just lowered it down from the heavens like the New Jerusalem. But I can assure you it didn't happen that way. It happened one prayer, one dollar, one committee meeting, one overcome obstacle at a time. It happened because, from the day of its founding until today, people sacrificed to make it happen. And the same is true of your church.

The true evidence that genuine sacrifice has taken place is when those who were involved say, "I'd do it all over again in a heartbeat." Just as a mother returns to the birthing room time after time to sacrifice to bring forth new life, so does everyone who experiences the blessing of setting aside time, treasure, and talent for God. When people are sorry they gave up something for God, you know it was done grudgingly. The absence of the willingness to continue to sacrifice is evidence of the absence of the blessing.

Those of us who stand for Christ today do so because of the sacrifice of those who came before us. And if there are going to be those who stand for Christ tomorrow it will only be because we sacrifice for Christ today. The cause of Christ is always only one self-centered generation away from failure, humanly speaking. All it takes is for one generation of Christians to make themselves the focus of their own life, to be more concerned about their own needs than the needs of others.

Everything we sacrifice for God on earth becomes part of our treasure laid up in heaven where we will enjoy the benefits of it forever. We never give up anything in this life that God doesn't repay many times over.

1. Read Genesis 4:1–8.

   a. Identify the two people who offered history's first sacrifices to God, and what they gave. (verses 2–4)

   b. What was God's response to each of the sacrifices? (verses 4–5)

   c. For what reason do you think God did not look favorably on Cain's sacrifice?

   d. What was Cain's reaction to God's response? (verses 5, 8)

e. What sacrifice did God make on Adam's and Eve's behalf in Genesis 3:21?

f. Why is there no record of humans offering sacrifices until Genesis 4? (What happened in Genesis 3 that changed everything?)

g. If sacrifice means devoting something to God, what *didn't* Adam and Eve devote to God in Genesis 3 that required the human race to begin sacrificing to God in Genesis 4?

h. If man was wholly devoted to God, why would no sacrifice be needed?

i. How does Mark 12:30 picture what Adam and Eve failed to do in Genesis 3?

2. Why is it necessary for Christians to continually offer themselves as a living sacrifice even though Christ became a sacrifice for our sins? (Romans 12:1)

    a. What kinds of actions (sacrifices) should be evident in the life of a Christian who lives as a living sacrifice?

    b. Using an Old Testament animal sacrifice as a parallel, can there be such a thing as a partial sacrifice? Why does the idea of a living sacrifice suggest a complete sacrifice? (How does Romans 6:1–7 correlate with Romans 12:1? In what way did we die, only to be raised to live as a sacrifice?)

3. Read Matthew 19:28–29.

    a. What reward awaits those who follow Jesus as His disciples? (verse 28)

b. And what reward awaits all who follow Christ in this life? (verse 29)

c. List the kinds of sacrifices Christ mentions that might be made in order to follow Him. (verse 29)

d. What does "hundredfold" refer to in verse 29. Is that number to be taken literally or figuratively?

e. List the sacrifices you have made to follow Christ as a Christian, or to follow God's particular call on your life.

f. Why do you feel the sacrifices have been worth it? In what way is the reward of heaven a just compensation ("hundredfold") for what you have devoted to God?

g. Identify any areas of sacrifice that you have struggled to make. What is the root of the struggle?

h. In what way(s) do you seek to live your life as a living sacrifice to God? (Romans 12:1)

DID YOU KNOW?

In the Old Testament, the sacrifice of an animal took the place of the believer. Hands were laid on the animal by the priest, transferring the guilt of sin from the believer to the animal, and then the animal was slain as a sacrifice devoted to satisfying the just requirements of God's holy law. In the New Testament, the sin of the believer was transferred to Jesus Christ who was then slain as a sacrifice devoted to satisfying (propitiating) God's wrath against sin. The Christian then is asked to give up himself not as a dying sacrifice, but as a living one (Romans 12:1) to serve God in spiritual acts of worship and service (Philippians 4:18; Hebrews 13:15–16; 1 Peter 2:5).

THREE DIMENSIONAL GIVING

John 12:1–11

In this lesson we see the difference between selfless giving and selfish stealing.

OUTLINE

An effective way to shine fresh light on any subject is to contrast it with that which is its opposite, a technique used in Scripture. The beautiful example of giving provided by Mary is made more clear when contrasted with the dark response by Judas.

I. Mary: The Positive Principles of a Giving Heart

A. A Sacrificial Attitude

B. A Servant Attitude

C. A Submissive Attitude

D. A Scriptural Attitude

E. A Serious Attitude

F. A Spiritual Attitude

II. Judas: The Negative Principles of a Greedy Heart

A. A Deceitful Attitude

B. A Dishonest Attitude

C. A Disobedient Attitude

One of the best ways to learn truth is to do character studies in Scripture, and one of the best ways to do character studies is to look at one person's life in relation to another—to see truth as it is revealed in contrast. For example, the generosity of Abraham is made plainer when we compare and contrast it with the self-centeredness of his nephew Lot.

In the following text, we will see the benevolence and love of Mary contrasted with the greed and selfishness of Judas Iscariot. It's easier to see Mary for who she is when Judas reveals who he is.

The context of John 12 is that it follows the dramatic and draining events of John 11—the resurrection of Lazarus from the dead. The Jewish leaders grew even more hostile toward Jesus after the event with Lazarus in Bethany: "Then, from that day on, they plotted to put Him to death" (John 11:53). So Jesus left Bethany and went with His disciples to Ephraim (John 11:54) and from there, six days before the Passover, they went to Jerusalem for the Passover (Mark 10:32). On the way Jesus stopped at Bethany to see Lazarus (John 12:1). The events we will study in this lesson took place at a dinner held in Jesus' honor in the home of one Simon the Leper (Mark 14:3).

MARY: THE POSITIVE PRINCIPLES OF A GIVING HEART

We can learn more about a giving heart from Mary than almost any other person in the Bible.

A Sacrificial Attitude

The gift that Mary gave to God was a "very costly" oil (verse 3). It was a sacrifice for her not only because it was expensive but because she set it aside for Jesus. The value of the oil is highlighted by what Judas said when he saw what Mary was doing (verse 5). He asked why the oil wasn't sold for three hundred denarii and the money given to the poor.

In Matthew 20:2 we learn that a denarius was one day's pay in Jesus' day. So when Mary dedicated something worth 300 denarii to Jesus, she was giving the equivalent of 10 months of wages (30 days × 10 months = 300 denarii). There is no question that this was a sacrificial offering on Mary's part.

I have heard of churches asking their members to consider giving a day's wages, and even a week's wages, as a gift for a special project.

And it would no doubt be a sacrifice for many today to give that much over and above their regular giving. But I have never heard of a church asking people to consider a gift of 10 months of their wages. But that's what Mary gave. Even though she had just buried her brother, Lazarus, a few days before this dinner, she had not even used this costly oil for him. Instead, she gave it as a sacrificial gift to Jesus.

Mary gave the very best she had to Jesus instead of something that was left over. That is the first principle of a giving heart.

A Servant Attitude

Many people had come to Jesus to receive from Him—healing, teaching, comfort, or wisdom—but Mary came to give to Jesus. Rather than coming to be served, she came to serve. She worshipped Jesus, and He commended her for it.

I have learned as a pastor to expect that when the phone rings or someone knocks on the door, they need something. And that's the way it should be. As a servant-leader, I am called to give—to serve the needs of the flock in whatever way I can. But there are those occasional times when the phone rings and someone says, "Pastor, I was just praying for you, and I thought I would call to let you know that I am standing with you in prayer for the effectiveness of your ministry. I don't need anything—just wanted you to know that I love you and am praying for you." Wow! What that does to a pastor's heart is indescribable. And that's what Mary did for Jesus. By her actions she was saying, "I love you, Lord." She came to serve her Lord.

A Submissive Attitude

The way Mary served the Lord illustrates the next principle: a submissive attitude. Just as Jesus would later demonstrate His own humility by washing the feet of His disciples (the act of a household servant), so Mary demonstrated her humility by bowing low and anointing the feet of Jesus with the oil. In addition, she let her hair fall down and used it to wipe his feet. For a woman to loose her hair in public was considered the practice of an immoral woman, and Mary demonstrated that she didn't care what others thought. Her goal was to serve her Lord regardless of the consequences.

Matthew and Mark note that Jesus' head was anointed whereas John refers to the anointing of His feet. Since Jesus took Mary's acts as preparation for His burial (John 12:7), it is likely that she anointed both His head and His feet.

A Scriptural Attitude

Mary did not give to Jesus because of high-pressure tactics. Rather, she gave to Him because she believed what He had been saying about His coming death, burial, and resurrection. In other words, she gave because she believed the Word of God spoken by the Son of God. Even the disciples had not fully comprehended and believed Jesus' words about His coming death. Her anointing was a response to His words. If Jesus was going to die, she responded by symbolically anointing Him.

Somehow Mary was one of the few who sensed the approaching hour of Jesus death. She sensed the hostility of the Jewish leaders and was determined to demonstrate her devotion to Him in light of the coming darkness that would envelope His life. Mary didn't care that no one else knew or understood—she acted on what she knew to be true.

A Serious Attitude

Mary was a serious follower of Christ. She saw a window of opportunity to minister to Him and she took it. Jesus said that the poor would always be with them, but He would not be (John 12:8). Had Mary waited, she would have missed the opportunity to serve and worship the Lord.

After Jesus was buried in the tomb following the Crucifixion, the next morning a group of women came to anoint Jesus' body for permanent burial. But they discovered the body was missing—Jesus had already been raised from the dead, and those women missed the opportunity to show their love and respect for Jesus in His death. Mary was determined not to miss that opportunity while He was still alive and anointed Him while she could.

Many Christians put off serving God, waiting for a "better" opportunity or for things in their lives to be less complicated. They wait until they aren't working as much, or until their children are grown and out of the house, or until they get out of debt. Then, they say, they'll begin giving to the Lord not only their money but their time and commitment. Before they know it, their whole life has passed by and they haven't done a thing.

If any of us waited until things were perfect in life, we wouldn't do anything. If we waited until we could afford to get married or have children, we'd all be single and the human race would stop growing. It's the same with giving to the Lord. We do the things that are necessary and right because often we only get one opportunity.

A Spiritual Attitude

Mary saw something spiritually that Judas totally missed. Mary was investing for the future, whereas Judas wanted to spend for the present. She didn't know it, but Mary's spiritual and sacrificial act of worship would be memorialized in Scripture for all to see: "Assuredly, I say to you, wherever this Gospel is preached in the whole world, what this woman has done will also be told as a memorial to her" (Matthew 26:13).

Arno C. Gaebelein, in his commentary on the Gospel of Matthew, wrote this about Mary: "Mary's act has come down to us in the gospel record coupled with His blessed name. None can read the Gospel without reading also the memorial of her personal devotedness. Empires have risen and flourished and passed away into the region of silence and oblivion. Monuments have been erected to commemorate human genius, greatness, and philanthropy. And these monuments have crumbled into the dust, but the act of this woman still lives, and it shall live forever. The hand of the Master has erected a monument to her which shall never, no never, perish."

JUDAS: THE NEGATIVE PRINCIPLES OF A GREEDY HEART

Having looked at Mary, it's time now to look at Judas. Examining his life will make Mary's wonderful qualities shine all the brighter. Mary is the example of what we should do and be, and Judas is the opposite. Just as we ought to follow Mary's example, we ought to flee from Judas's.

A Deceitful Attitude

At first it could appear that Judas had something noble in mind—selling something and giving the money to the poor. After all, we would find Barnabas doing the same later in the early church (Acts 4:36–37). But John adds this explanatory note concerning Judas's request: "This he said, not that he cared for the poor, but because he was a thief, and had the money box; and he used to take what was put in it" (John 12:6). Judas didn't care about the poor. He wanted the costly oil to be sold so the money could be put into the disciples' money box from which he would then help himself, removing it over time.

Just as Mary left a memorial to herself, so did Judas. The name Judas had been popular in Jewish culture prior to the time of

Christ—Judas Maccabeus was a great hero of the Jews during the Jewish revolts in the time between the Old and New Testaments. But since Judas Iscariot's betrayal of Christ, rarely do we find anyone, Jewish or Christian, named Judas. His name is forever associated with deception and betrayal.

A Dishonest Attitude

Besides being deceitful, Judas was dishonest. He wanted people to think he was someone that he was not. I have seen many instances as a pastor of people using external pious behavior to try to cover up a life of carnality. I recall once when our church had just completed part of a building project and many of the church members had gathered to help do the final cleanup before the building could be used. And I learned about an individual who, though he was there working, was saying to others the same thing that Judas said about Mary's gift of perfume: "We shouldn't have spent this money on a church building given how many poor and needy people there are in the world." I was not surprised when I learned of his remarks because I knew him to be a person who was not, shall we say, generous toward the Lord or others. He was guilty in his own life of that of which he accused others—of misusing God's money. But he used a pious façade to cover up his own shortcoming, just as Judas did.

This is not so much deceitful as it is dishonest. It is not living one's life honestly before others. The J. B. Phillips translation of the New Testament actually uses the word "dishonest" to describe Judas: "He said this, not because he cared for the poor, but because he was dishonest." Judas resented Mary's sacrificial offering because he would like to have had the money for himself. It was no accident that Judas's final act was to sell Jesus for thirty pieces of silver. Judas's betrayal of Jesus was not a moment of weakness, it was an act of dishonesty consistent with his hunger to acquire money. Judas was a thief, a dishonest man, and he sold the Savior for silver.

The last book in the Old Testament contains a haunting question from God spoken by the prophet Malachi: "Will a man rob God?" (Malachi 3:8) And when it is asked, "In what way have we robbed You?" the answer comes back, "In tithes and offerings." When we fail to give to God what is rightfully His, but conduct our lives as if we are wholly committed to Him, there is a measure of dishonesty about us.

A Disobedient Attitude

Once a minister of the Gospel was trying to impress upon a man his obligation to be obedient to God's Word. When he asked the man if he'd ever been baptized, the man said, "No, I haven't. But why should I? The thief on the cross was never baptized and he went to heaven." The minister then stressed the importance of being faithful in church attendance. "Why should I attend church?" the man asked. "The thief on the cross never went to church and he went to heaven." The minister then pointed out the need to be faithful in giving to the Lord. "Why should I give anything?" the man said. "The thief on the cross never gave a penny and he went to heaven." Turning away, the minister said, "Sir, the only difference I can see between you and the thief on the cross is that he was a dying thief and you are a living one."

And he was an honest thief; he accurately described his behavior. And the minister did the right thing by not trying to twist the man's arm to make his behavior conform to an external standard. Giving, along with other true spiritual disciplines, has to come from the heart. But there is a necessity for confrontation—for people to hear what their responsibilities are from the Word of God. Without knowing what God expects, we will never be likely to do it.

There is no way to cut corners on what God expects to be done. We hear the Word of God, and then we choose the response we will make—to be like Mary or to be like Judas. And our legacy, as with each of these two, will follow us when we're gone. I believe many more Christians would begin to give as God expects if only they were confronted by the plain teaching of the Word of God. It is never a matter of asking, "How can the church raise more money?" We are not a social service organization that has car washes and bake sales to raise money. When we obey Him in the matter of giving, there will be no shortage of money.

Will you be a Mary or a Judas? What you decide to do with the resources of the Lord will ultimately reveal your choice.

1. Read 2 Samuel 24:18–25.

   a. What did the prophet instruct David to do to stem the plague that was afflicting Israel? (verse 18)

   b. How did David intend to get the threshing floor? (verse 21)

   c. What offer did Araunah make to David? (verses 22–23)

   d. Why did David reject Araunah's offer? What did he do instead? (verse 24)

   e. What comparison can you draw between David's philosophy of giving to the Lord and Mary's actions in John 12:3?

   f. Why is cost inherent in the concept of sacrifice?

g. In what way is there little or no cost represented in the offerings described in Malachi 1:13–14?

h. What cost might be a reality for those who follow Jesus? (Matthew 19:29)

i. What different kind of cost is associated with Jesus' words in Luke 14:26–27?

j. What costs have you encountered as a follower of Christ? To what degree have you made them gladly? How often do you find something other than gladness entering the equation?

k. Is there any area in which you are giving God less than the best you have to offer? What keeps you from giving the best?

2. Describe how Barnabas was a positive example of what Judas recommended in John 12:5. (Acts 4:37)

    a. How were Ananias and Sapphira guilty of the same base motivation that characterized Judas? (Acts 5:4)

    b. How did Judas lie about his proposal? (John 12:6) What did he plan to do with the money?

    c. How did Ananias lie to the apostles? What was his sin? (Acts 5:2, 4)

    d. Who was Ananias probably trying to emulate by his deception? (Acts 4:36–37)

    e. Which is the greater sin in your opinion—being honestly selfish or deceitfully generous?

3. When Jesus ate the meal (John 12:1–2), what was Martha's role? (verse 2)

a. How is the same "division of labor" between Martha and Mary in this setting also seen in Luke 10:38–42?

b. Describe the activities of the two sisters on that occasion?

c. How did Jesus describe both their behaviors? (verses 41–42)

d. Both the sisters made sacrifices for Jesus. Describe the sacrifice each made?

e. Why is giving Jesus our personal attention and fellowship more valuable to Him than our works?

f. What was it in Mary that Jesus was drawing attention to? (verses 40–42)

g. Did she seem to be making her sacrifice (giving her gift) cheerfully of grudgingly?

DID YOU KNOW?

The "oil of spikenard" Mary used to anoint Jesus was an extract from the roots and stems of the *Nardostachys jatamansi* plant that grows in the Himilayan region of India. (The "spike" part of the name was in reference to the plant's shape.) It was mentioned in the context of King Solomon's reign in the Song of Solomon 4:13–14, undoubtedly imported into Israel from India as part of Solomon's extensive commercial trading enterprises. The fact that the oil came from such a distance was the basis for its great expense. Added to that fact was the powerful and desirable room-filling fragrance of the oil. It was normally used only to anoint those in positions of high honor. (From *Eerdman's Dictionary of the Bible*.)

GOD'S HARVEST LAW

2 Corinthians 9:6–15

*In this lesson we discover why giving is
a form of sowing that leads to reaping.*

OUTLINE

God has built laws into His kingdom. We sow a seed in the ground
and are rewarded with hundreds in return—more than we need,
more to plant again. The same is true for the replication of spiritual
life. We sow and God provides a harvest—more than we need,
more to sow again.

I. **The Principles of God's Harvest Law**
   A. The Principle of Investment
   B. The Principle of Identity
   C. The Principle of Increase
   D. The Principle of Interval

II. **The Products of God's Harvest Law**
   A. We Prosper Spiritually and Financially
   B. We Prove Our Love for God
   C. We Provide for Those in Need
   D. We Provoke Many Thanksgivings to God
   E. It Promotes Prayer on Our Behalf
   F. We Purchase Greater Opportunity to Give Again

III. **The Perfect Example of God's Harvest Law**

R. G. LeTourneau was a Christian businessman who died in 1959 and is remembered as a pioneer in the development and building of heavy construction equipment that was used the world over. Today, LeTourneau University, a biblically-based interdenominational Christian university in Longview, Texas, is a legacy to R. G. LeTourneau's commitment to God's harvest law.

LeTourneau learned to obey God's harvest law the hard way. During the difficult days of the Great Depression in the 1930's, his company made $35,000 profit in its first year. He decided to hold back his $5,000 commitment to his Christian and Missionary Alliance church and invest the money back in the business, believing he would then have even more to donate the following year. But God was not mocked, LeTourneau used to say. The next year he lost $100,000 and felt thoroughly chastened for withholding the Lord's tithe from the previous year. He committed himself to pay back to the Lord the money he had withheld, plus more—and his whole life changed.

Within four years of making that commitment, he and his wife formed the LeTourneau Foundation with 90 percent of the stock of the LeTourneau Corporation. At one time the Foundation's holdings amounted to $40 million, the earnings from which financed Christian work all over the world.

R. G. LeTourneau used to say, "It is not how much money I give to God. It is how much of God's money I keep for myself that matters." He also said in an interview with a famous business publication, "There are two things I like to do. One is to design machines, turn on the power, and see them work. The other is to turn on the power of the Gospel and see it work in peoples' lives." He did well in both categories. At the time of his death, he held more than 200 patents for machinery inventions. And besides giving up 90 percent of his income to Christian work, he flew all over the world to speak for the Lord on the benefits of following God's stewardship principles. He became the only man ever to have been the president of both the Christian Businessmen's Committee International and the Gideons International at the same time.

R. G. LeTourneau proved the accuracy of God's harvest law found in 2 Corinthians 9:6: "But this I say: He who sows sparingly will also reap sparingly, and he who sows bountifully will also reap bountifully."

THE PRINCIPLES OF GOD'S HARVEST LAW

There are four principles that make up the whole of God's harvest law: investment, identity, increase, and interval.

The Principle of Investment

This principle says we reap only if we sow. If I hold in my hand a single kernel of corn, I hold a marvelous reproducing agent. If I plant that single kernel in the ground and nurture the plant that comes up to maturity, I will harvest many hundreds times more kernels than the single one I planted. I can then replant some of those kernels and the cycle repeats itself indefinitely.

But suppose I become so enamored with the wonder of that little kernel that I decide, instead of planting it, I will frame it in a lovely frame and set it on my mantel so I can admire it for the rest of my life. Every time I walk by, I can say, "My, what a beautiful kernel of corn! What amazing potential that kernel of corn has!"

If I do this, the kernel will never reproduce, never bear fruit. In order for that kernel to return anything to me, it has to be planted in the dirt and nurtured to maturity. In other words, we only reap if we sow. This is the principle Jesus enumerated in John 12:24: "Most assuredly, I say to you, unless a grain of wheat falls into the ground and dies, it remains alone; but if it dies, it produces much grain."

From the perspective of the financial resources God has entrusted to us, if we refuse to sow God's seeds into the field of His kingdom, there will be no return. We reap only if we sow, whether in agriculture or in financial stewardship. And with the sowing comes the joy of the Lord—the joy of seeing God's resources return a harvest that glorifies Him and builds His kingdom. The lack of sowing into God's work may be one of the reasons there are so few wealthy people who have found true happiness. Andrew Carnegie, one of America's richest men, once said, "Millionaires who laugh are rare."

The blessings God intended for man come only from sowing that which He has entrusted to us. We will not reap the blessing if we hoard that which we have been given.

The Principle of Identity

This principle says, in addition to getting *when* we sow, we get *what* we sow. If we plant corn, we will get corn, not barley. That which we sow is what we reap. Galatians 6:7 says, "Whatever a man sows, that he will also reap." Paul also says if we sow to the flesh, we will reap the corruption of the flesh; but if we sow to the Spirit we will reap the everlasting life of the Spirit (Galatians 6:8). Sometimes when I hear someone remark about how unloving people are, I immediately wonder if that person is reaping exactly what he has sown. I love to be around joyful and positive people because as they sow their seeds of joy into my life, I become a harvest field in which joy springs up as well.

It pays to sow the kinds of attitudes and behaviors you would like to see more of in our world. If you sow faith and joy wherever you go you will reap a harvest of faith and joy from your actions. That's the principle of identity in God's harvest law.

The Principle of Increase

In addition to *when* and *what*, the principle of increase says I get more than I sow. Think about what agriculture would be like if a farmer planted one kernel of corn and four or five months later harvested a corn stalk and found only one new kernel: a one-to-one ratio of sowing to reaping! We would all starve to death if that were the case. There is a built-in principle in God's economy that we harvest more than we sow.

Second Corinthians 9:10 says that God will "multiply the seed you have sown and increase the fruits of your righteousness." Luke 6:38 says, "Give, and it will be given to you: good measure, pressed down, shaken together, and running over will be put into your bosom. For with the same measure that you use, it will be measured back to you." A harvest that is "running over" is the result of sowing according to the principle of increase.

Over and over Paul uses the word "abundance" in 2 Corinthians to drive home the fact that when God returns a harvest, it is an abundant harvest (8:2; 9:6, 8, 11, 12). God is not a miser! He is a generous God who repays the faithful sower with a generous harvest. He likes nothing better than to bless with abundance the one who generously sows into His kingdom. God wants us to have "an abundance for every good work" (verse 8), and He provides in accordance with the principle of increase.

The Principle of Interval

This is the principle that covers the place where most Christians stumble in their financial stewardship. The principle of interval says that we get later than we sow.

Suppose the farmer goes to the field, puts his kernel of corn in the ground, covers it up, waters it, goes home to have lunch, and then tells his wife he's going back to the field to check on the corn crop he planted that morning. He comes back and tells his wife he's not sure this farming thing is going to work out: "I planted the corn, but there's nothing coming up."

Well, that sounds a little ridiculous, but it's an exaggerated example of how we treat our financial sowing sometimes. I've had many, many Christians report to me that after beginning to give of their finances to God, a week later they hadn't seen any harvest. They wondered why the law of the harvest wasn't working. Nobody expects to sow and reap on the same day, or in the same week, in the natural world. Yet somehow in the spiritual world (the supernatural world), we expect to sow one day and reap a great harvest the next. Not so—there is an interval between sowing and reaping in the spiritual world just as there is in the natural world.

My father was a pastor in two churches in Ohio before being called to become the first president of Cedarville College in the same state. The college began with ninety students and no money, and both my parents invested themselves thoroughly in that school for twenty-five years. There was never a great financial harvest for them as a result of their spiritual sowing, nor did they expect there to be. But after my father retired from that position, he and my mother could travel all over America and reap a harvest of blessings from twenty-five years of sowing into the lives of thousands of students. That harvest was slow to come, especially in the beginning; but it increased every year so that by the time they retired, their barns were full of spiritual fruit. If you had asked them, "Was it worth the investment for two-and-a-half decades, they would have said, emphatically, 'Yes!'" There is an interval between the time we sow and the time we reap the harvest.

Three verses document this principle:

- Galatians 6:9 "In due season we shall reap if we do not lose heart."
- Ecclesiastes 11:1 "Cast your bread upon the waters, for you will find it after many days."
- Hebrews 6:10 "For God is not unjust to forget your work and labor of love which you have shown toward His name."

God does not forget seeds that are sown. Ask any farmer or gardener—seeds germinate at different rates. Some germinate quickly and some more slowly. Then the rate at which they bear fruit is different. And it is the same in the spiritual kingdom of God.

THE PRODUCTS OF GOD'S HARVEST LAW

Now we need to look at six products of God's harvest law—exactly what the results are when we sow in faith.

We Prosper Spiritually and Financially

Verses 8–11 of 2 Corinthians 9 say God makes all grace abound to us, and we have sufficiency and an abundance that we are "enriched in everything for all liberality." That is the result of sowing abundantly into the kingdom of God. It's a law! This is not something I'm making up—it is the promise of the Word of God. God himself stakes His name and reputation on this promise to prosper those who sow in faith.

We Prove Our Love for God

Paul says in verse 13 that we prove ourselves by our obedient giving. And back in chapter 8, verse 8, he told the Christians that he was testing the sincerity of their love by sharing with them about the diligence in giving by the Macedonian churches. When we give to God, we demonstrate the reality and the level of our commitment to God. It's one thing to say, "I love God," but it's another to sacrifice for Him. When our sacrificial walk doesn't match our spiritual talk, the latter is called into question.

We Provide for Those in Need

Verse 12 says that when the Corinthians gave, they would be supplying the "needs of the saints" in the church in Jerusalem. And we do the same when we give. Many churches have benevolence funds out of which they minister to the needs of members and others who have needs above and beyond their own ability to meet. Whether we give through our church or give directly, sowing financially is one way we provide for those in need.

We Provoke Many Thanksgivings to God

Notice the chain of events in verse 11: When we give to the Lord, He liberally enriches us in everything in return, and that "causes thanksgiving through us to God." Verse 12 continues, saying that "many thanksgivings to God" abound. And Paul expresses his own thanks for the grace of God in them that provoked them to give (verse 15). Every dollar you give to the Lord eventually results in praise to His name.

It Promotes Prayer on Our Behalf

Paul says in verse 14 that those who are the beneficiaries of our sowing in turn pray for us, thanking God for using us to bless them and asking God's blessing on us in return. So our giving sets off the chain-reaction of spiritual activity that might otherwise never have occurred. You may never know what blessings come to you through the prayers of those who receive the benefits of your gifts.

We Purchase Greater Opportunity to Give Again

One of the reasons God blesses us when we give is so that we will have the ability to give again. The result of our giving is God blessing us with an abundance (that means more than we need) "for every good work." If we have more than we need, we can continue to give to God for the spiritual and material benefit of others. Just as a farmer has plenty of extra corn kernels to replant the next year, so God blesses us with enough to continue to give. As God supplies "seed to the sower" (verse 10), He supplies an abundance for us.

THE PERFECT EXAMPLE OF GOD'S HARVEST LAW

There is no better example of God's harvest law than the way God followed that law himself. When God was faced with a fallen human race and the prospect of redeeming them to spend eternity with Him, I picture Him (in human terms) contemplating how to achieve the goal of "bringing many sons to glory" (Hebrews 2:10). If the goal was to "harvest" many sons, He knew the law of harvest required Him to sow a son. And so the method of redemption was for God to sow His own Son into the field of planet earth. He died and fell into the earth (John 12:24) for three days and then sprang to life and returned to heaven, bringing many spiritual sons with Him.

I believe that's what Paul is thinking of in verse 15 when He says, "Thanks be to God for His indescribable gift!" Specifically, he's referring to the grace of God in the Corinthians that moved them to give. But the evidence of that grace is how He sowed His own Son into sinful humanity so He could reap an eternal harvest of souls.

I pray that you will take God at His Word and prove the law of harvest in your life.

1. Read 2 Corinthians 8:13–15.

   a. What misconception was Paul guarding against in verse 13a? (What is one tempted to think when giving sacrificially to others?)

   b. What is the goal Paul describes in verse 14?

   c. Is the goal of equality an ongoing one in "Christian" economics, where those who have an abundance should give to those who have less until all have the same amount? Or is this for "emergency" situations only, so that none perish out of want when there are others who have an abundance?

   d. What is the difference between communism where equality is forced and Christianity where equality is voluntary?

   e. How does voluntary sharing turn out, in time, to result in blessing for those who give? (verse 14)

2. Read 2 Corinthians 9:6–15.

   a. To whom does "he" refer in verse 6? That is, does God's law of harvest apply to non-Christians in any way? Seeds planted by non-Christians produce crops, so does money sown by non-Christians result in a harvest? Why or why not?

b. Should Christian ministries accept financial gifts from non-Christians who give willingly and cheerfully with what knowledge they have? Why or why not? (verse 7)

c. God provides enough seed for the farmer to _____ and enough to make _____ to eat. (verse 10a) Explain how this translates to financial giving: God will provide enough money for you to _____ to others and enough money to _____ on.

d. To what is "righteousness" referring in verse 10? How is giving generously an indicator of righteousness? What does Psalm 15:2, then verses 3–5 add to your understanding? How does giving generously fit with the characteristics listed there?

e. Are you in a position to give generously "in all liberality" ("on every occasion," NIV) (verse 11)? If that is God's intent (verse 11a), what would it take for you to get to that place?

f. What are the two things that happen when we give generously? (verse 12)

g. Explain how giving is evidence of one's confession of belief in the gospel of Christ? (verse 13)

h. Conversely, what does failing to give do to one's confession of Christ?

i. What does the phrase "sharing with them and with all men" mean? (verse 13) Should Christians give not only to Christians but also to non-Christians who are in need? What are some examples of the latter type of giving that would confirm one's confession of Christ.

j. Did Jesus examine those to whom He ministered theologically before giving to them? How should our giving follow His example in being generous "with all men"?

DID YOU KNOW?

M any commentators believe that Paul's statement in 2 Corinthians 9:6—"He who sows sparingly will also reap sparingly"—is his quotation or paraphrase of a well-known proverb. It is not a direct quotation of a biblical proverb, however. Since all economies were agrarian in biblical days, the concepts of sowing and reaping were well known. Just as well known was the relationship of sowing to reaping in terms of quantity— sow sparingly, reap sparingly; sow abundantly, reap abundantly. There are a number of Old Testament passages that reflect these universal truths: Proverbs 11:18, 24–25; 19:17; 22:8–9; Hosea 8:7; 10:12.

WHEN WE FORGET GOD

Haggai 1:1–15

In this lesson we discover what happens when we focus on ourselves with our money instead of on God.

OUTLINE

It's a battle to keep priorities straight. Because failures usually happen gradually, we sometimes have to step back and consider the big picture to realize what we've done. That's what Haggai counseled Israel to do when they failed to maintain their financial priorities before God.

I. The Excuse

II. The Exhortation
   A. Consider Your Ways
   B. Go and Do

III. The Encouragement
   A. God's Presence Is Always Available
   B. God's Power Is Always Available

Everyone has had the experience of having more month than money, of looking around at the end of the month and discovering that there are still bills to pay. When we combine inflation, costs that rise faster than wages, and our insatiable lifestyle desires, it's not unusual today to find people, maybe even ourselves, running out of money before all our needs are met or bills are paid.

Five hundred years before the time of Christ, the same situation characterized a group of Jews to whom Haggai addressed his prophetic message. They worked and earned, but it was never enough. It was as if, the prophet said, they had money bags with holes in them (1:6). The money seemed to just flow like sand through their fingers. These were the Jewish settlers who had returned to Israel from the Babylonian captivity.

Haggai told the people that the reason this was happening was that the temple of the Lord stood in ruins. The people had been constructing their own houses but had left the house of God untouched (verse 9). A little background is necessary to understand this problem.

The people of Judah, the two southern tribes of Israel, had been in captivity in Babylon for seventy years. After Babylon was conquered by Persia, the Persian king, Cyrus, gave permission for the Jews to return to Israel, reinhabit their homeland, and rebuild their temple. According to Ezra 2:64, there were 42,360 Jews who left Babylon and returned to begin work on the temple that had been destroyed by Nebuchadnezzar.

The temple was a sacred place for the Jews. Our churches today are not like the Jewish temple. Our churches are meeting places; but there was only one temple, and it was the place where God dwelt in the Holy of Holies above the ark of the covenant to meet with the High Priest—the place where the Shekinah glory (from Hebrew *sakan*, to dwell) of God resided. For seventy years this singular cite of worship for the Jews had lain in ruins.

The initial enthusiasm to rebuild the temple was high when the Jews returned to the land of Judah. They cleared a place and laid a fresh foundation for the altar of sacrifice that stood directly in front of the temple proper. There were no walls for the sanctuary itself or surrounding the courtyard, but the altar was in place. Ezra 3 says that the people celebrated enthusiastically when the altar was restored. But soon the enthusiasm subsided.

This is the natural order of things, of course. Many of us can remember how excited we were when we first became Christians only to be surprised when our enthusiasm waned. We discover in many areas of life that starting well is easier than finishing well. Young converts who were going to save the whole world, in time find themselves unwilling to bow their head and pray before a meal in a restaurant for fear of being identified as a Christian.

It's easy for the luster to wear off, and that's what happened to the Jews after they had been home a short time. Ezra 4:24 says the work stopped, and we learn from reading Ezra that it was because of local opposition that rose up against the Jews from their neighbors. These neighbors obviously didn't want Jews moving back in and claiming the right to the land and to Jerusalem. But king Cyrus of Persia had declared it, so the Jews were protected by his decree. Nonetheless, the Jews used the political wrangling as an excuse to stop work. The altar was in place, but nothing else.

Now enter Haggai, a prophet who minced no words when it came to speaking for God. Haggai was a preacher who, to use modern terms, let it all hang out. He took no prisoners when he preached. He fired both barrels and made no excuses. He put the cookies on the bottom shelf where everybody could get them.

In this passage of Haggai's message, we're going to find that he makes three points: the excuse, the exhortation, and the encouragement.

THE EXCUSE

Verse 2 of the opening chapter of Haggai's prophecy begins with a complex set of quotations that essentially say this: The people of Israel were saying that it just wasn't the right time to complete the rebuilding of God's house. That was their excuse—the timing wasn't right. The temple needed to be finished, but now is not the right time. It's amazing to read this excuse of theirs and realize how common it is. I have heard the same excuse from people in our day and time.

It seems apparent from verse 6 that it was harvest time in Israel. The people felt it was better to return to the fields and harvest the crops so they could survive than to give priority to God's instruction to rebuild the temple. So "not the right time" translated to "we don't have time." The tendency to put off, to procrastinate, when it comes to God's work is widespread. We're always looking for a more convenient time to do what we know we should do now.

I don't know of another realm in which the excuse of "I'll get to it someday" is heard more often than in financial stewardship. By that I don't mean just giving a little money here and there to the Lord on Sunday, but a full-orbed recognition that all we have is His and that our recognition of that fact is returning to Him a tithe and offerings from what we have been given. People say, "I know I need to do that, and I plan to as soon as I get my finances a bit more in order. I plan to do that soon, but not now."

I have talked to too many Christians through the years not to believe this is the line of reasoning. But what happens is this: People with the "timing" excuse never find the right time. There's always a reason not to begin giving faithfully to God.

THE EXHORTATION

Haggai's exhortation—his response to their excuse-making—begins in verse 3. He begins with a slightly sarcastic tone by referring to the time they'd spent building their own "paneled houses." They didn't have time to build God's house but apparently had had time to build their own while the temple lay in ruins.

The houses the people were building were not just plain houses but paneled houses, finished with luxurious wood beams and panels on the inside. After Nebuchadnezzar's siege against Jerusalem, there were few forests in the immediate area, so wood had to be imported from other regions. They were going to significant trouble and expense to build very nice houses for themselves.

The people had forgotten why God allowed them to return to their land. It wasn't to enrich themselves first—it was to restore God to a central place in the life of His chosen people, the temple being the primary indicator of that central place. They had gotten distracted after their initial burst of enthusiasm and had started investing in themselves rather than in God. They were using money that belonged to God to build comfortable lives for themselves. All they had done for God was to erect an altar upon which sacrifices could be offered. They then turned aside from this bare-minimum approach to rebuilding the temple to build their own comfortable houses.

Starting in verse 5, Haggai says some things that most preachers today wouldn't dare say. He points out to them their insatiable quest for more: You sow, but reap little; you eat and drink but are never satisfied, you clothe yourselves but are never warm, you put your money in a bag with holes in the bottom. They were infected with the inflation virus, the desire for more which is never satisfied. They were accumulating for accumulation's sake; and since starting down that path, they had not reached a place of contentment or fulfillment.

In verse 9, Haggai identifies the cause of their financial problems: "Because of My house that is in ruins, while every one of you runs to his own house." They thought they would get ahead, enabling them to return to God's priorities by tending to their own priorities first. They directed all their own energy and resources to themselves; but they remained totally unsatisfied, and their needs remained unmet.

Everyone who commits to be faithful to the Lord in financial stewardship has times where it just doesn't seem like it will be possible to remain faithful—our family has certainly experienced that tension. Yet somehow when we remain faithful to our priorities to give to the Lord first, He causes everything to work together and every need to be met. But if we stop giving to Him, eventually everything else gets out of order as well.

The old Southern preacher said it this way: "When God gets His, and I get mine, then everything's just fine. But if I get mine and take God's too, what do you think God will do? I think He'll collect. Don't you?" I believe that He does. Haggai was saying to the people of Israel that they could not take what was God's and spend it on themselves. Eventually they would find themselves lacking for everything.

Haggai gave his people a two-step action plan.

Consider Your Ways

Verse 5 contains the first step: "Consider your ways!" The challenge from the prophet is to step away from the trees and look at the forest—consider your actions and look at the big picture results. "Am I better off by failing to obey God than I would have been if I had obeyed Him all along?" The answer for the Israelites was obviously, No.

Every Christian today needs to ask himself the same question. Am I struggling financially because I have failed to honor the Lord from the first of all my resources? Is it possible I am constantly playing catch-up because I don't break the cycle and begin honoring God with my money? It's possible to go year after year without stopping to consider our ways—to take stock of our situation and the reasons for it. Every Christian needs to evaluate what he is doing against God's template for financial stewardship. It's not always a comfortable assessment to make. But most growth involves change, and most change is uncomfortable. So we would be wise to stop and consider our ways.

Go and Do

The second action step Haggai gave them is in verse 8: "Go up to the mountains and bring wood and build the temple, that I may take pleasure in it and be glorified." Haggai was telling them something we need to hear as well: Don't debate this any longer. Just go get the wood and begin to build the Lord's house. Don't discuss timing and reasons pro and con; just do what you know the Lord wants you to do."

For them, they needed to begin immediately since they hadn't done anything in a long while. But for those who have been giving regularly to the Lord for many years, the same step applies. Don't get casual, don't be tempted to relax, don't think you deserve a break. Keep your stewardship commitment as an active topic of discussion in your home. Each year, at least, sit down together and make a commitment to continue or increase what you have been giving to the Lord.

The bottom line in Haggai's message was, "Don't just consider your ways. Consider your ways and then act! Fix what's broken and do what needs to be done."

THE ENCOURAGEMENT

After focusing in on their excuse, and delivering an exhortation, Haggai gave the people a word of encouragement: "I am with you, says the Lord" (verse 13). And the people responded. The Lord moved Zerubbabel and Joshua to lead the people to return to their work on the house of the Lord (verses 14–15).

There are two powerful lessons in Haggai's word of encouragement and the peoples' response.

God's Presence Is Always Available

First, God is always available to provide wisdom, encouragement, and blessing to those who will choose to obey Him.

When we look at the money and the month and can't see how it's possible to make them match, we should ask God for help. He is always there to provide wisdom when we find ourselves struggling between the rock of our will and the hard place of His (James 1:5). God has never asked His people to do something that He has not provided resources to accomplish. If you put the numbers down on paper and they don't match up, ask God to show you how He can make it work as you remain faithful. The promise is, "I am with you, says the Lord."

God's Power Is Always Available

Implicit in the promise of God's presence is the promise of His power. Haggai uses a wonderful term to describe how the Lord moved the people to begin working again: "So the Lord stirred up the spirit of Zerubbabel . . . and the spirit of Joshua . . . and the spirit of all the remnant of the people" (verse 14). Somehow God began to move the people to do the work. We don't know how He stirred them up, but He did. It appears from the text that their actions came first. I have found in my own life that if I wait until I "feel like" something is right, I never act. But if I act first, the feelings of conviction and confirmation will follow. Many of the convictions I hold dear in my life are things I don't "feel like" doing. But after I do them, I always feel glad that I did.

The principle is this: What God instructs me to do, He will equip me and empower me to do. God's presence is available, and His power is available for everyone who decides to do His will.

We cannot reverse our priorities! That's what the Israelites had done—the opposite of Matthew 6:33. In that verse, Jesus says to seek first the kingdom of God and everything else will be added to us. They were seeking "everything else" first instead of the kingdom of God, and they found themselves in want. God knows what we need in this life and promises to provide it when we keep our priorities straight by seeking Him first.

God is God and so deserves to be first. One way of proving to Him that we understand this is by putting Him first with everything we have. It's a discipline that He recognizes as a choice we have made, and He rewards that choice by blessing us with more of His resources to manage.

Wherever you stand in your own commitment to God, stop and consider your ways. Let God prove His presence and power to you by making real that which seems impossible.

1. Read Matthew 6:25–34

   a. What is the theme of this bit of teaching from the Sermon on the Mount? (verse 25)

   b. In a day when most people were self-employed and had no "benefits," was Jesus touching on unusual worries of a few or standard worries of most? In that case, to what degree do His words apply to you?

   c. How does verse 34 and verses like Deuteronomy 10:18 and 1 Timothy 6:8 summarize all of life's needs into two basic categories? What are they?

   d. What does Paul say about our desires for more than these two needs? (1 Timothy 6:8)

   e. What point is Jesus making in verse 26 about God's ability to provide?

   f. What point do you think Jesus is making in verse 27 with regard to adding to one's "stature"? (Looking at other Bible translations may give you ideas.)

   g. Regarding the two categories of necessities, which is covered in verse 26 and which in verses 28–30?

h. In what way should believers be different from non-believers in how they procure the necessities of life? (verses 31–32)

i. How should the believer arrange his priorities in life? (verse 33a)

j. How would you describe what it means to seek the kingdom of God and God's righteousness?

k. When we make God's kingdom a priority, what does Jesus promise that God will then do? (verse 33b)

l. Why is it a waste of time to worry about tomorrow? What do you really know about what tomorrow will hold? (verse 34)

m. Based on what you have learned so far in this study guide, what will characterize the financial activities of a person who is seeking God's kingdom first in his life?

n. Conversely, what will likely characterize the person's financial life who is seeking his own "kingdom" first instead of God's?

2. What promise did Paul make to the Philippians in Philippians 4:19?

   a. Based on the Philippians' actions, how did they qualify for the promise of Jesus in Matthew 6:33? (Philippians 4:10–18) Whose kingdom were they seeking?

   b. What other promise does Paul make concerning his ability, through Christ, to do the will of God? (Philippians 4:13)

   c. How might that apply to the ability to give faithfully and generously to God?

3. Read Deuteronomy 30:1–16.

   a. How do verses 11–13 approximate the heart of Haggai 1:1–15 in terms of the people making excuses about not doing God's will?

   b. How does verse 11 cut through all the excuses? Why does obeying God in giving ultimately come down to a matter of obedience?

DID YOU KNOW?

Palestine of antiquity, unlike today, was once covered by thick forests. The Old Testament is filled with many references to the forests that existed in that period (Deuteronomy 19:5; 2 Kings 19:23; Isaiah 10:34; Jeremiah 10:3; Zechariah 11:2). Lebanon, in the north, was where the most coveted trees for building grew. Solomon contracted to have the cedars of Lebanon brought to Jerusalem for the construction of the temple (1 Kings 5:6). Cedars were brought from Lebanon for the rebuilding of the temple after the return from captivity (Ezra 3:7). Haggai's command to Israel to go "up to the mountains" to get wood is not likely referring to Lebanon but to what wood could be gathered locally (Haggai 1:8).

GIVERS AND TAKERS

Genesis 13–19

In this lesson we learn the difference between being generous and self-centered in this life.

OUTLINE

We have all known people who seem to go through life giving money and things away, whether it's picking up the check for a meal or supporting missionaries on the field. Giving for them is a lifestyle and a life-cycle: the more they give, the more God seems to give to them.

I. Lot, the Taker
   A. Lot Became Interested in the Wrong Direction
   B. Lot Became Insensitive to God's Voice
   C. Lot Became Incompatible with Himself
   D. Lot Became Inevitably Involved in Sin

II. Abraham, the Giver
   A. Abraham Gave Away What He Had
   B. Abraham Gained Position at Home
   C. Abraham Gained Prosperity for His Family

A powerful yet simple quotation from the Lord Jesus Christ, one found nowhere in the four gospels, occurs in Acts 20:35: "It is more blessed to give than to receive." The word "blessed" in Greek (*makarios*) means fortunate, or happy, which puts this saying of Jesus totally at odds with modern culture. The world would say one is more fortunate or happy if he receives, not if he gives. But in the kingdom of God, the more one gives, the more blessed (fortunate and happy) one becomes. As with all kingdom truth, we have to take this by faith: Understanding will follow obedient practice.

The world is divided up between givers and receivers (or takers). The Bible provides illustrations of those who spend their lives giving for the benefit of others and those who spend their lives taking from others. The former are others-centered and the latter are self-centered. Barnabas would be a good example of a giver, while Ananias would be an example of a taker (Acts 4:36–5:11). Mary, the sister of Lazarus, was a giver, while Judas Iscariot was a taker (Matthew 26:6–13). As we noted in an earlier lesson, seeing these pairs in the same context provides an amazing contrast by which to evaluate each.

Is it more blessed to give than to receive, or is that just a truth that has been turned into a religious platitude by the well-meaning since Jesus first uttered the words? In this lesson we study another pair: Lot, the taker, and Abraham, the giver.

LOT, THE TAKER

Lot came with his uncle Abraham out of Mesopotamia. He had the opportunity to become a giver—he became wealthy from his association with Abraham. He had numerous herds and livestock and servants and was in a position to be-come a person who blessed others through his possessions. But he came to a crossroads in his life where he had to make a decision whether to remain with Abraham or to become independent.

He and Abraham's herdsmen were beginning to fight one another. Instead of staying with Abraham and working out a way to share the land and wealth with his uncle, Lot struck out on his own to try to increase his wealth. His demise, spiritually and then physically, is well documented in Scripture. We see the results of choosing to become a taker instead of a giver.

Lot Became Interested in the Wrong Direction

In Genesis 13, we read that Lot became interested in Sodom. Many times spiritual downward spirals begin when we take our eyes off the Lord and put them on the things of the world. And for Lot it was the sinful city of Sodom that lured him away. Lot left Abraham and pitched his tents near Sodom.

Sodom, of course, is the source of our English word sodomy, a word referring to perverted sexual practices which is what the city was known for. Genesis 13:13 says that "the men of Sodom were exceedingly wicked and sinful against the Lord" (see also 2 Peter 2:7–8; Jude 1:7). It was this place that Lot chose instead of staying with Abraham. He gave up the opportunity to grow and develop and share in the blessings of God toward Abraham.

Lot is not the only person to have made a wrong decision in that regard. Any Christian can be walking with God and begin to look around and see something that looks like it might be more fun or more interesting than the kingdom of God. That person takes his eyes off Christ and finds himself drifting away. That's the first step in becoming a taker.

Lot Became Insensitive to God's Voice

When we become enamored with the things of the world, we begin to tune God out—we become insensitive to His voice. And that's what happened to Lot. Two incidents in Lot's life illustrate what happened.

After Lot became assimilated into the life of the city of Sodom, a coalition of kings came against the city and captured a number of the inhabitants including Lot and his family. Word got back to Abraham that his nephew had been captured by these leaders. Any other man might have been justified in a "serves him right" kind of attitude toward Lot. After all, Lot had taken the best land available when Abraham gave him first pick for new land to live on. And now he was in trouble? "Serves him right," some people might have said.

But not Abraham. He gathered his servants and military men and went after the men that held Lot. He rescued his nephew and his family by defeating the kings and gave Lot and his family their lives and freedom back. Well, freedom of a sort. Instead of allowing this incident to serve as a wake-up call, Lot took his family and went straight back to Sodom. Instead of making a break with a way of life that almost cost him and his family their lives, Lot decided to keep serving himself and his own interests by going back to the wicked city of Sodom. That was his second major step in affirming his identity as a taker instead of a giver.

We can see Lot's insensitivity to God's voice a final time when God tried to rescue Lot before the destruction of Sodom (Genesis 19). Even in the midst of being rescued, Lot was arguing with God. It's amazing how stubborn we can get when we become takers instead of givers.

Lot Became Incompatible with Himself

In 2 Peter 2:6–8 we get a picture of Lot's continual devolution as a taker. Peter tells us that Lot was "oppressed by the filthy conduct of the wicked" in Sodom and "tormented his righteous soul from day to day by seeing and hearing their lawless deeds . . . ." Lot thought he was going to make himself wealthy by moving to Sodom and getting involved in its commerce and culture, but all around was filthy unrighteousness. I believe deep in Lot's soul there was a desire to please God, but he was consumed by his appetite for wealth and materialism. He became incompatible with himself. He was now a tormented soul, an unhappy and miserable man. Intent on grabbing all the gusto he could from the world, Lot became a divided man. That was Lot's third step in becoming a taker.

Lot Became Inevitably Involved in Sin

Lot's life was a downward spiral as illustrated by his increasing involvement with the city of Sodom. First, he pitched his tent near Sodom so he could see the city. The next time we meet him, he's living in the city. In his final appearance, we find him sitting with the elders in the city gate—the place of government. This was his fourth self-centered step—to become a leader in a wicked city. It's a small step from sanctioning sin in the life of others to participating in that sin oneself.

The last picture we have of Lot is his committing incest with his daughters after having escaped God's destruction of Sodom. He participated in the same perverted sexual immorality that Sodom was known for when he first pitched his tents on the outskirts of the city. In a drunken stupor he fathered children by his own daughters—daughters he had offered to the men of Sodom for their own sexual pleasure a short time before.

Lot's life was a downward spiral of bad choices that led him to become the ultimate self-gratifier. In contrast with Lot, however, was his uncle, Abraham, who lived his life as a giver.

ABRAHAM, THE GIVER

As a result of being a giver, Abraham gained position for himself and prosperity for his family.

Abraham Gave Away What He Had

Abraham was apparently responsible for giving Lot his start in life. Abraham took his nephew under his wing and gave him a start in "the business." Eventually Lot's holdings in livestock became so large that he and Abraham's flocks and servants were getting in each others' way. Abraham took the initiative to propose that they move farther apart and offered Lot the option of choosing where he wanted to go. "Choose whatever part of the land you desire," Abraham told Lot, "and I'll take what's left."

It would have been appropriate for Lot, given their history, to have responded, "Uncle Abraham, I wouldn't have any-thing if it weren't for you. You deserve to have first choice. That's the least I can do to pay you back for all you've given me. You choose first and I will take what's left." Instead, Lot chose the best land he could find, which happened to be on the plains in the direc-tion of Sodom. And God's response to Abraham was to give him the entire land of Canaan (Genesis 13:14–18).

Abraham had a history of giving. He paid tithes to Melchizedek after defeating the coalition of kings. He was gracious toward the king of Sodom after defeating the kings. He was gracious toward Hagar when she left Abraham's camp. Abraham had a generous spirit as opposed to Lot who had a greedy spirit.

God continually blessed Abraham as you will see while we follow the path of his life. He stumbled on a couple of occasions but never lost his generous spirit. God gave him land, descendants, and bless-ings as he lived his life as a giving person.

Abraham Gained Position at Home

Abraham continued to grow and be enlarged in his position both in public and in his home. In Genesis 18:19, we find one of the greatest testimonies to a father I have ever read anywhere: "For I have known him, in order that he may command his children and his household after him, that they keep the way of the Lord, to do righteousness and justice, that the Lord may bring to Abraham what He has spoken to him."

Compare this statement with how Lot ended his life: living in a cave, in a drunken stupor having sexual relations with his own daughters. On the other hand, God is saying about Abraham that he will lead his family to keep the way of the Lord and do righteousness and justice. Who do you think prospered the most—Abraham or Lot? Is it better to be a giver or a taker?

I have sat and wept with businessmen who spent their lives trying to gain everything they could materially only to find that they lost their family in the process. That's what happens when we live life as a taker. We ultimately reap what we have sown. A psychiatrist who came to know Christ through our church's ministry wept as he told me about the lives of sin his children were leading. He had lived an ego-driven life to become wealthy and had lost his children. What hurt him the most was that his children were living a life that they had learned from him. He wished he could go back and live his life all over again.

Abraham Gained Prosperity for His Family

Abraham not only prospered *in* his family, he gained prosperity *for* his family. As for land, we've already seen that God gave Abraham far more land than what he lost to Lot. But more important than land was his relationship with the Lord. Genesis 13:18 says that Abraham moved near Mamre ("fatness" or "blessing") near Hebron ("communion") and built an altar (a picture of fellowship) to the Lord. Abraham kept his family together, gained land and prosperity for his family, and kept his relationship with God intact—whereas Lot did the opposite.

If we were to put Lot's life on a ledger sheet—to see what he gained and lost—here is what it might look like:

Gains	Losses
All of the wealth of Jordan.	The companionship of Abraham.
A home in the rich and aristocratic city of Sodom.	A place near Hebron; the fellowship of God.
Friendship with the Sodomites.	Communion with God.
Influence in the city of Sodom.	Influence in his own home.

I would say that Lot gained nothing and lost everything. When Lot tried to get his family out of Sodom before God rained judgment on it, his children and their spouses thought he was crazy. He wasn't even able to influence his own children! Some of his immediate or extended family probably perished in the destruction of Sodom because Lot had no credibility with them.

We need to apply the differences between Abraham and Lot to the subject of stewardship, and the primary application is this: The way we respond to the temptation of materialism will determine whether we become a giver or a taker in life. Abraham was a giver who prospered, while Lot was a taker who perished.

First Timothy 6:10 says, "For the love of money is a root of all kinds of evil, for which some have strayed from the faith in their greediness, and pierced themselves through with many sorrows." And Paul's next words to Timothy are words that Lot would have been wise to have heeded: "But you, O man of God, flee these things and pursue righteousness, godliness, faith, love, patience, gentleness" (verse 11). Had Lot fled the source of his temptation, Sodom, he might have changed the course of his life and become a giver like his uncle Abraham. Instead, the love of money was too great, and he perished at the end of the downward cycle he began by not fleeing "these things."

It's obvious that wealth was not the problem because Abraham and Lot were both wealthy. Paul doesn't say it's "money" that is the "root of all kinds of evil," but "the love of money." In an earlier lesson in this study guide, you were introduced to R. G. LeTourneau, a very wealthy man who lived on 10 percent of his wealth and dedicated the remaining 90 percent to the furtherance of the Gospel. So it is possible to be wealthy without yielding to the temptation to become materialistic. Abraham passed that test, but Lot failed.

I don't know who wrote this prayer, but it is well suited to close this lesson on givers and takers: "Eternal God, tie me to something eternal. I tie myself to things—to houses, to land—but some twist of fate robs me of them. I tie myself to love, but one microbe takes my loved one out of my life forever. I tie myself to a friend who then ceases to understand me. Tie Thou me to truth, ageless like Thyself. Tie Thou me to a purpose, endless like Thyself. Tie Thou me to work, the life-long Savior of heart and hands and brain. Tie Thou me to human need, for thereby Thou hast redeemed many. Tie Thou me to Christ who said, 'Abide in me.' Tie Thou me to Thyself, who failest not."

1. How does Proverbs 11:24 represent a paradigm for the lives of Abraham and Lot?

2. What do you learn about the source of all wealth from the following verses?

    a. Deuteronomy 8:18. Why was the issue raised in this context?

    b. Proverbs 10:22. To what is wealth connected in this verse?

    c. Ezekiel 16:19; Hosea 2:8. How does God's wealth sometimes ironically get used?

    d. Genesis 24:35. Where did this man learn his perspective on wealth?

    e. Genesis 26:12. To whom did Abraham's blessing extend?

3. Read Matthew 19:16–30.

    a. Summarize the dialogue between the man and Jesus in verses 16–20.

    b. What additional instruction did Jesus give him? (verse 21)

    c. How did the man respond, and why? (verse 22)

    d. How did the man's response verify the principle Jesus stated in verses 23–24?

    e. What did Jesus mean by the statements in verses 23–24? Why is it hard for the wealthy to get to heaven?

    f. What light does Matthew 13:22 shed on this question?

g. Why do you think Jesus told the man to sell everything he had? Should all wealthy people do this? Was this a test for the one individual or a principle for all?

h. Jesus' reaction to the disciples' astonishment at His saying seems cryptic. What did He mean in verse 26? (Hint: Rather than the man who walked away being unusual, isn't he like all of us, unable to save ourselves? Is this a word about God's grace? Explain.)

i. What was Peter trying to prove with his bold statement in verse 27?

j. Instead of rebuking Peter for his self-congratulatory statement, what assurance did Jesus give him? (verses 28–30)

3. In the final analysis, is it necessary to give up everything to be saved? (Ephesians 2:8–9)

a. Will God ultimately repay that which has been given up to follow Jesus? (Matthew 19:28–30)

b. In light of that truth, why is Matthew 6:19–20 good advice?

c. Jesus doesn't _____ us to give up everything, but neither are we told _____ to if that's what we choose to do. There is no _____ on what we can give to God.

4. Fill in the rest of this popular saying about money that is based on 1 Timothy 6:7: "You can't take ____ _____ _____."

a. What does Paul say happens to those who desire to be rich? (1 Timothy 6:9)

b. How is the first part of verse 10 often misquoted in popular culture?

c. Why does "the love of" change the entire meaning of the verse?

DID YOU KNOW?

In ancient times, a city gate was the place where the elders or officials of the city met to conduct business. The gates were not simply doors set into the walls of the city. Given that the walls of ancient cities were very thick, the "gates" of the city referred to the room-like interior portion of the city walls where there was room for a group to gather. Ancient walls still standing today, for example, surrounding the Old City of Jerusalem, still reflect this architecture. Jesus used the term "gates" as a metaphor for the scheming efforts of the leaders of hades to prevail over the church.

GIVING TOO MUCH

Exodus 35–36

In this lesson we see what happens when stewardship is orchestrated by God and His people respond.

OUTLINE

Someone has said that God's purposes, carried out in God's way, will never lack God's supply. If that's true, why do many churches and ministries struggle financially? It is not because God created a project too big. It's because God's people have not fulfilled the role given to each one.

I. God Was Responsible for the Need

II. God Was Responsible for the Giving

III. God Was Responsible for the Offering
    A. It Was a Freewill Offering
    B. It Was a Revelatory Offering
    C. It Was an Offering unto the Lord
    D. It Was an Inclusive Offering

IV. God Was Responsible for the Inspiration

V. God Was Responsible for the Glory
    A. God Had a House
    B. God's People Had a Hope
    C. We Have a Great Story

Did you hear about the young Mexican boy who showed up at the official U.S. border crossing several times a week? He would approach the crossing on a bicycle and always had two bags of sand slung over his shoulder. The guards were suspicious, of course, that some type of contraband might be concealed in the bags of sand. Even when they made him empty the bags out, they could find nothing and were always forced to let him through. One day, however, one of the border patrol agents ran into the young man in a restaurant and struck up a conversation. He finally convinced the young man to tell him what he had been smuggling into the United States on the promise he wouldn't press charges. And the young man said, "Bicycles. I was smuggling bicycles."

That story reminds me of how easy it is for us to miss that which, in hindsight, is plainly obvious. And that can happen when we consider the subject of stewardship. The first thing we think of when considering stewardship is preachers telling us to give more money to the church. That's because it's what we "see" with our mind's eye when the subject is first raised.

But that's a case of seeing only what is on the surface, what is plain. First and foremost, stewardship is not about money. Stewardship is about the heart. Money is only the outward manifestation of the condition of the heart. Like the officers who were so focused on sand that they couldn't see the bicycles, we can be so focused on money that we fail to see the real issue in stewardship: the condition of the heart.

The event we will look at in this chapter, found in Exodus 35–36, is a perfect place to study how the heart should respond to the opportunity to give to God. The setting is the building of the tabernacle as Moses was leading the children of Israel from Egypt to the Promised Land.

Some scholars have estimated that if the Jewish tabernacle were to be constructed today, it would cost upwards of ten million dollars. That amount (adjusted backward to Moses' day) represented a large sum for a group of people who had just been rescued from slavery! Yet the amazing thing that happened is that Moses had to stop the people from bringing resources to the "tabernacle fund." The people gave more than enough. (When's the last time you heard of a church building campaign that told its members, "Stop giving! We have enough!")

GOD WAS RESPONSIBLE FOR THE NEED

The first point to make is to remember who was responsible for this need: God was. The tabernacle wasn't Moses' idea, it was God's. He had created, through Abraham, a people for himself and had kept them protected and isolated in Egypt for 400 years while they grew into a nation. They entered Egypt as seventy members of Jacob's family and came out as several million. God wanted a place to meet with His people and so commissioned Moses to build the tabernacle.

This seems like a basic principle, but churches would do well to remember it today. The church of Jesus Christ is God's idea, not man's. If we don't remember that, we can begin to associate the funding of the church with the need to fund a man's vision or a man's ministry. That is a huge mistake! The church and its ministry are God's and His alone. And the money for that ministry must be thought of in that context.

The godly pastor who preceded me at the church where I am the pastor was a true visionary. Not only did he build a great church, he had a vision for Christian education which led to grammar and high schools and even a four-year Christian college. I am fully convinced that this broad ministry was not his idea, but that God gave that vision to a man He knew would receive it and implement it. As he shared that vision with those in the church at that time, they responded; and the vision was carried out over a period of years, and continues to expand today. The source of the vision and the ministry makes a big difference when it comes time to fund that vision. The buck stops on God's desk, if you will, when we attempt to carry out the mission of the church. It is His idea. And the same was true when it was time to build the tabernacle in the wilderness.

GOD WAS RESPONSIBLE FOR THE GIVING

It stands to reason that if the project of the tabernacle was God's idea, the way to pay for it would have to be His idea as well. God knew He was going to ask Moses to build a very expensive structure in the wilderness, and He also knew that the people who would have to pay for that structure had been slaves for the previous 400 years. In other words, there was a huge expense and no one with any money! This was not a surprise to God, and the answer to this dilemma had been incorporated into the plan all along.

In Exodus 11:1–3, we find God spelling out the plan to Moses. First, God was going to bring ten plagues on the Egyptians. Second, He was going to set the Hebrews free. And third, the Hebrews were to ask the Egyptians for money on their way out of town. The Egyptians were probably so glad to see the Hebrews (and their plagues) leave Egypt that they loaded them down with gold and silver, fine materials, and other valuables. In Exodus 12:35–36 we see the plan working—when the Hebrews left Egypt, the Egyptians "granted [the Hebrews] what they requested."

So when it came time to build the tabernacle in the wilderness, it was built with Egyptian money! Long before the need became a reality, God had worked out a way for it to be paid for. When it came time for the money to be given, it was in Jewish hands. But God had put the money in His people's hands before the need was made known.

This is a powerful lesson for God's people today, both for churches and for individuals. Many individual believers don't want to begin giving faithfully to God because they don't think God will meet their needs by allowing them to pay their bills. And churches engage in all manner of worldly fundraising activities because they think it's up to them to raise the money for a particular project. But what God directs to be done, God is faithful to fund. Our challenge is to be obedient and trust Him to provide money for what He has told us to do.

GOD WAS RESPONSIBLE FOR THE OFFERING

God created the need, and God arranged for the financing. And when it came time to collect the money, He initiated the offering as well.

It Was a Freewill Offering

Exodus 35:5 tells us that when Moses called for funds to be brought, he asked only those who were willing to participate in the offering. And that's the way it happened: "Then everyone came whose heart was stirred, and everyone whose spirit was willing, and they brought the Lords' offering for the work of the tabernacle . . ." (verse 21; see also verses 22, 29). Four times in this passage reference is made to the offering being a voluntary event. In other words, those that came forward with an offering did so voluntarily because they wanted to. No coercion or pressure or direct mail campaign— just a desire to see a dwelling place for God be built.

It Was a Revelatory Offering

God made it perfectly clear to each person what he was to contribute to building the tabernacle (35:10). Moses furnished a list of all the things that needed to be crafted (verses 11–19) and invited all the artisans in the community to come forward and apply their skills. Every individual had an assignment to fulfill.

I believe that is a valid principle for today as well. We should ask the Lord to show us what part we are to play in funding the work of His ministry and then trust Him to reveal that part to us. God knows the present as well as the future, and so He might tell us to do something like the Macedonian Christians did—give beyond our ability (2 Corinthians 8:3). But we have to ask Him in faith to tell us what our part is to be and then trust Him to provide the ability for us to fulfill that part. He may speak to us through His Word or in prayer, but He will guide us if we ask Him in faith.

It Was an Offering unto the Lord

Besides being a freewill and revelatory offering, their offering was also unto the Lord. Regardless of who we give our money *through*, we always give it *to* God. Over and over in Exodus 35, it is emphasized that the offering was to be for the Lord (verses 5, 21, 22, 29). There were no fundraising or capital campaign organizations in the wilderness, and the Hebrew slaves themselves had no organizational structure except for Moses and Aaron. So it was clear to the people that they were giving to God. While that fact can get lost today, it shouldn't. God is the object of our giving.

Sometimes people get upset about how some organization is using their money and they think, "I'll show them," and they redirect their funds in some other direction. That shows a misplaced focus. Our money does not go to organizations; it goes *through* them *to* the Lord.

It Was an Inclusive Offering

Often in the Old Testament, we hear more about men than we do the women. But when this offering was taken, verse 22 says, "They came, both men and women, as many as had a willing heart." Everyone participated in helping to build the tabernacle in the wilderness. Everyone had been given wealth by the Egyptians, so everyone participated in bringing that wealth to give to God.

In a large church like the one I pastor, we have diverse demographics. It would be very easy for some of our college students or single parents to think, "God doesn't expect me to give since I'm on such a limited income." But I believe God has a part for everyone to play. We should never make the assumption that we are exempt from giving time, talent, or treasure to God because we have little money. Remember—God knows the future. He may have money He wants you to give even though He's not given the money to you yet!

The reason no one should be excluded from participating is so that no one will be excluded from the blessing. Giving is an individual act, not a corporate act; and if churches are going to be blessed, it will be because individuals are blessed.

GOD WAS RESPONSIBLE FOR THE INSPIRATION

Three times in Exodus 35–36 we find the word "stirred" (verses 35:21, 26; 36:2). The people were motivated by an outside force, that force being God himself as He stirred the peoples' hearts to give. As a result of God inspiring the people to give, the people brought much more than was necessary (36:5): "The material they had was sufficient for all the work to be done—indeed too much" (36:7). What we are learning from this incident in the wilderness among a bunch of previously poor people is that God's work will never lack provision when it is done God's way. When all of God's people participate, there will be more than enough to accomplish God's will.

A problem occurs when God's vision is grasped by leaders and members, and people vote to accomplish the mission—but they vote with their hands, not their checkbooks. And the former is easier than the latter. The latter vote takes faith to implement, but sometimes the faith doesn't catch up with the vision and financial tension occurs. I believe that when the people of God respond to the inspiration of God, there will never be a gap between the vision and its accomplishment. But when, as is true in many churches, only a minority of the people are obediently tithing to God, there will be a delay. And with delay comes doubt and discouragement. That happens because the people of God have not responded to the inspiration of God.

GOD WAS RESPONSIBLE FOR THE GLORY

Because God created the need and the supply and inspired the offering, the results were glorifying to Him.

God Had a House

There they were in the middle of the desert, not a building or tent or town in sight—and all of a sudden God had a house! Seemingly miraculous things happen when stewardship is overseen by God.

The first church I pastored started with seven families meeting in four mobile homes put together in an L-shape. The two trailers where we met for church had the interior walls removed so it would seat about a hundred people, and the other two trailers were used for Sunday school classes. The church grew and we had people packed in everywhere in those trailers. I remember the day, after the church service, that we marched out of those trailers and into our first new building. It was wonderful! And then a few years later, after holding double services in that building, we marched into a new building that would seat 1,200 people. Each time we made a move, it was because God had ordained the plan and provided the resources and inspiration, and people gave willingly.

Based on how we felt, I can imagine how Israel must have felt when they built God a house in the middle of the desert.

God's People Had a Hope

The tabernacle became a symbol of hope for the Israelites— a reminder that God was dwelling in their presence. We can have that same hope today when we see God give the church a vision, provide the resources, and work in peoples' lives who obey His leading. It's a supernatural thing when people give sacrificially instead of spending their money on themselves. It's a sign of hope, a sign that God is with us.

We Have a Great Story

Finally, we have a story of victory that parents tell their children for generations, a story in which God was the playwright, producer, and director and they were the actors, a play that the world looks at with envy and wonders how it happened.

I encourage you to play the role God gives you in the next stewardship story He orchestrates for His glory. I assure you that you are written into the divine script. It only remains to be seen whether you will answer the call.

APPLICATION

From Exodus 35–36, answer the following questions about the conception and funding for the tabernacle in the wilderness.

1. How does verse 35:5 parallel and perhaps inspire Paul's message in 2 Corinthians 9:7?

2. What do you think would happen to Christian giving if only the believers who gave willingly/cheerfully gave to the Lord?

3. How willing/cheerful are you about your giving to the Lord? If you feel any manner of compulsion or pressure to give, from where does the pressure come?

4. Do you think it's better to give even if your attitude isn't perfect than not to give at all? Which do you think God values most?

5. List in groups of similar items the various things the people had with them to give. How does this list illuminate Exodus 11:3 and 12:36?

6. What does the variety of objects say to you about the variety of things people can give to the Lord in addition to money?

7. For people who have little treasure, how could their time and talent supplement their treasure in contributing to a church project?

8. How often do you hear this kind of contribution being made possible in church giving today?

9. Outline the three steps in the funding process for the tabernacle:

Step 1: (verse 35:5)

Step 2: (verse 35:20)

Step 3: (verse 35:21–29)

10. In which step do you find pressure to give being exerted by Moses?

11. What do you think the people were doing in Step 2? Based on the section in this lesson titled "It Was a Revelatory Offering," what could modern Christians do during this step in the process?

12. Besides Bezalel being a craftsman (verse 35:30), what else did Moses call him to do along with Aholiab? (verse 35:34) Remember that most of the Hebrews had been slaves making bricks and were "unskilled" laborers. How could this concept of training the willing (verse 36:2) be implemented today in church stewardship projects?

13. How are verses 36:5–7 a good background for Ephesians 3:20? How normal should this kind of occurrence be in Christian stewardship projects today? Why do you think we rarely hear of anything like this?

14. What happened when the construction of the tabernacle was complete? (Exodus 40:34–35)

15. How would you summarize this project from conception to completion as an example of how Christian "fundraising" ought to work in the modern church?

DID YOU KNOW?

The tabernacle, like the temple that followed it, was tripartite in design, as were the temples of many pagan religions: an outer court, an inner holy place, and a final most holy place. Pagan religions had an image of the deity in the inner sanctum, but Israel's tabernacle had no image, consistent with the second of the ten commandments (Exodus 20:4). The wood used in building was acacia wood, acacia being the only tree that grew in the desert, indicating that the account of the tabernacle was written by Moses at that time. The most expensive and colorful materials were used closest to the most holy place. (*From the Dictionary of Biblical Imagery.*)

Turning Point
Resources
By Dr. David Jeremiah

Stewardship Is Lordship

Believers who give their lives and resources demonstrate Lordship. When we choose to make God the Lord of every area of our lives, He promises to respond with more grace. The more open our lives are to give, the more God is able to give to us.

Stewardship Is Lordship will guide you to a deep and practical understanding of how to give confidently and joyfully— and be blessed as a result of your obedience.

Study Guide SILSG *(Can - $12/UK - £6)* $10
Cassette Album SILAL (10 tapes) *(Can - $90/UK - £40)* $70
Compact Disc Album SILALCD (10 CDs) *(Can - $100/UK - £50)* $80

Great Offerings

Great Offerings explores lessons from the Great Tabernacle offering taken first by Moses and later by King David. These offerings are powerful examples for us to follow in our own giving.

Cassette Album GROAL (4 tapes) *(Can - $36/UK - £16)* $28

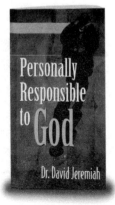

Personally Responsible to God

Stewardship is no small matter in the life of the believer. Jesus said, "Where your treasure is, there your heart will be also" (Matthew 6:21). In this booklet, Dr. Jeremiah examines six principles that will answer questions such as: "Why should I give?" "How should I give?" "When should I give?" You will be challenged to ask yourself, "Where is my treasure?"

Booklet PRGBL *(Can - $3.75/UK - £1.75)* $3

Turning Point
Resources
By Dr. David Jeremiah

Investing for Eternity

In this study, you will be challenged to let God's Word speak to you on the issue of money and Christian stewardship. You will study subjects such as grace giving, personal commitment, and the priority of your relationship with Jesus Christ. Most importantly, you will hear God's final answers about the biggest investment you will ever make—the investment for eternity.

Study Guide IFESG *(Can - $12/UK - £6)*   **$10**
Cassette Album IFEAL (10 tapes) *(Can - $90/UK - £40)*   **$70**
Compact Disc Album IFEALCD (10 CDs) *(Can - $100/UK - £50)*   **$80**

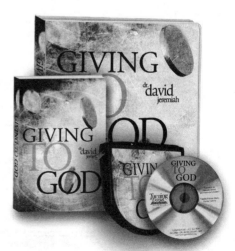

Giving to God

Biblical principles of stewardship lead us to harvest the blessing of faithful giving. *Giving to God* will help you explore what the Bible has to say about sowing, stewardship, and sacrifice. Coming to understand the promises in God's Word regarding your finances will not only change your pattern of giving, it will revolutionize your perspective of God!

Study Guide GTGSG *(Can - $12/UK - £6)*   **$10**
Cassette Album GTGAL (10 tapes) *(Can - $90/UK - £40)*   **$70**
Compact Disc Album GTGALCD (10 CDs) *(Can - $100/UK - £50)*   **$80**

Turning Point Resources

STUDY GUIDES

All Study Guides are regularly priced at $10

An audio album is also available for each of the following series.
(Sold separately. Individually priced.)

Acts: The Church in Action (2 Volumes)
Authentic Christian Life, The
   (1 Corinthians, 3 Volumes)
Blessings and Behavior of the Believer, The
   (Ephesians, 2 Volumes)
Captured by Grace
Celebrate His Love (Christmas)
Christians Have Stress Too
Christ's Death and Resurrection
Courage to Conquer
Escape the Coming Night
   (Revelation, 4 Volumes)
Facing the Giants in Your Life
Family Factor
For Such a Time as This (Esther)
Fruit of the Spirit, The (Galatians)
Gifts from God (Parenting)
Giving to God
God, I Need Some Answers
God in You (The Holy Spirit)
God Meant It for Good (Joseph, 2 Volumes)
God's Principles of Stewardship
Grace of Giving, The (Stewardship)
Greatest Stories Ever Told, The (Parables)
Handwriting on the Wall (Daniel, 3 Volumes)
Heroes of the Faith (Hebrews)
Home Improvement
How to Be Happy According to Jesus
   (The Beatitudes)
How to Live According to Jesus
   (The Sermon on the Mount, 2 Volumes)
Invasion of Other Gods (New Age)
Investing for Eternity
Issues of the Home and Family
Jesus' Final Warning (Prophecy)

Joy of Encouragement, The
Knowing the God You Worship
Learning to Live by Faith (Abraham,
   2 Volumes)
Living by Faith (Romans, 6 Volumes)
Living in the Light (1 John)
Looking for the Savior (Thessalonians,
   2 Volumes)
Miracles of Christ
My Heart's Desire (Worship)
Nation in Crisis, A (Joshua, 2 Volumes)
New Spirituality, The (New Age)
Overcoming Loneliness
People God Uses, The
People Who Met Jesus
Power of Love, The
Powerful Principles from Proverbs
Prayer—The Great Adventure
Ready! Set! Growth
Runaway Prophet—Jonah, The
Ruth, Romance and Redemption
Searching for Heaven on Earth (Ecclesiastes)
Seeking Wisdom—Finding Gold
Signs of the Second Coming
Spiritual Warfare
Stewardship Is Lordship
Tender Warrior, The (David, 2 Volumes)
Turning Toward Integrity (James)
Turning Toward Joy (Philippians)
What the Bible Says About Angels
What You Always Wanted to Know About
   Heaven
When Wisdom Turns to Foolishness (Solomon)
When Your World Falls Apart (Psalms)

BOOKS

Captured by Grace $20
Discover Paradise $15
Escape the Coming Night (Revelation) $13
Gifts from God (Parenting) $19
God in You (The Holy Spirit) $19
Grace Givers $15
Handwriting on the Wall, The (Daniel) $12
Joy of Encouragement, The $13
Life Wide Open (Purposeful Living) $19
My Heart's Desire (Worship) $19
Prayer—The Great Adventure $13
Prayer Matrix, The $10

Sanctuary (Daily Devotional) $14
Searching for Heaven on Earth (Ecclesiastes) $22
Secret of the Light, The $15
Slaying the Giants in Your Life $13
Things That Matter, The $10
Turning Points (Daily Devotional) $14
Turning Toward Integrity (James) $10
Turning Toward Joy (Philippians) $10
Until I Come (Prophecy) $13
What the Bible Says About Angels $13
When Your World Falls Apart (Psalms) $13
Why the Nativity? $10

POSTAGE AND HANDLING CHART

For orders	Add
Up to $5.99	$1.50
$6.00-$19.99	$2.50
$20.00-$50.99	$3.50
$51.00-$99.99	$6.00
$100.00 & over	$9.00

If you would like a complete catalog
of resources available from
Turning Point, please call
1-800-947-1993 or write
Turning Point ~ P.O. Box 3838 ~
San Diego, CA 92163-1838.
You can also visit Turning Point at
www.turningpointonline.org